# Everything Without Content 233

I0795678

Verlag der Buchhandlung Walther und Franz König, Köln

Photographs by Stefano Graziani

# De Carlo

## Experiments in Thickness

# Contents

# Experiments in Thickness

De Carlo at the planned opening of the 1968 Milan Triennale

The story goes that Giancarlo de Carlo's career started in the aftermath of his unsuccessful debut at what was effectively the last CIAM conference in Otterlo in 1959. In the slipstream of the frontal attack on his fellow Italian (and mentor) Ernesto Rogers' presentation of BBPR's Torre Velasca, De Carlo's own, slightly undercooked Matera housing project was in turn labelled conservative. The criticism of the Italian group (which also included Gardella and Magistretti) drew much from the article Reyner Banham had published a few months earlier on the 'Italian retreat from modern architecture'.[1] However, while the Torre Velasca was seen as flatly historicist, the Matera housing (admittedly a victim of unfortunate circumstances) was somehow deemed too modern, its orthogonal urban scheme still clinging to the newly outmoded CIAM ideology. According to Aldo van Eyck, De Carlo had failed to recognise that the picturesque old hilltop town was the paragon of the *casbah*—a much-loved catchword denoting something vague and non-Euclidean, an urban matrix of the multitude that was supposed to supplant the CIAM grid. This was an omission De Carlo would be sure to remedy when it came to that other picturesque hilltop town, Urbino.

In 1959 in Otterlo, Aldo van Eyck reigned supreme. He presented the Orphanage (which

1 Reyner Banham, 'Neoliberty: The Italian Retreat from Modern Architecture', *Architectural Review*, no. 747 (April 1959), 231–235.

was to become a harbinger of structuralism), he delivered a manifesto (illustrated by the *Otterlo Circles*), and he freely handed out copies of the relaunched *Forum* magazine (which was to become the unofficial publishing platform of Team 10). Van Eyck was responsible for everything in this first issue, from the content to the design of the cover. Spiralling out across the front of the magazine were a series of vague terms: 'cluster', 'imagination versus common sense', 'appreciated unit', 'identifying devices', 'aspects of ascending dimension', 'l'habitat pour le plus grand nombre'. Inside, a farrago of proclamations in different fonts (including Van Eyck's 'Aesthetics of Number') jostled with scenes from African villages and European cities, the whole infused with a general presentiment of something new—the issue ended with a mysterious nod to Le Corbusier: 'Vers une "casbah" organisée…' This was speaking in tongues, a tour de force many found inspiring—and confusing. By his own admission, De Carlo was 'deeply interested' in Van Eyck's ideas. This encounter has been credited for the 'radical shift' in De Carlo's architecture, from an embellished modernism—undoubtedly informed by the postwar reaction to Italy's complex struggle with the 'modernist style'—towards an architecture of clustered figures, conurbations and systems that make a claim to be 'urban', albeit in a modest way.

The next time his work came under the scrutiny of Team 10, Giancarlo de Carlo emerged triumphant. Six years later, in Berlin in 1965, he presented the Collegio del Colle, student housing for the University of Urbino, then under construction. Everybody seemed to agree this was 'a successful, innovative response to the issues that had been discussed within Team 10'. De Carlo's unlikely lifetime involvement with Urbino had begun in the early 1950s. He would become the de facto town architect, doing virtually everything from the masterplan down to the public lighting system. Over the course of nearly fifty years, he built no less than fifteen major projects, and the Collegio del Colle was the first of them. It ticked all the boxes. This time there was the casbah, as a small-city-large-house model adapted to the topography. There was the threshold (Van Eyck called it a 'threshold building'). There were the cells and the network. There was the infrastructure and a pattern of growth. There was no hierarchy. There were the intermediate spaces between the private and the communal areas where people were supposed to 'encounter and exchange experiences'. And there was history. But rather than the brute medievalism of the Torre Velasca, this took the form of a subtle affiliation to Francesco di Giorgio, up to then an overlooked—and therefore conveniently ripe for resuscitation—Quattrocento architect in the service of the Duke of Urbino, whose 'humanism and functionally imaginative formalism' De Carlo was able to identify with. The exposed brick and concrete structure sprawling over the hillside beyond the historical town, with its zigzagging clusters of residential cells connected by open pathways to the nucleus of common space, was the embodiment of Team 10 doctrine: identifiable, made of recognisable pieces, skeleton-like. Together with Aldo van Eyck's Orphanage, Candilis-Josic-Woods' Free University and Alison and Peter Smithson's Robin Hood Gardens, Giancarlo de Carlo's Urbino student housing would become a textbook illustration of Team 10, the palpable evidence of an idea.

Another project for student housing presented at the Berlin meeting was the 1964 competition entry for the university in Enschede by the Team 10 newcomer, Oswald Mathias Ungers. At first glance, this was also architecture as an urban form, not unlike De Carlo's project, but it met with a lukewarm reception. Ungers, too, was concerned with the 'greater number' and a growing population, and was likewise a proponent of collective spaces.

But didn't seem to share the 'good intentions' of his Team 10 counterparts. His language was that of morphology, typology and composition. 'In Enschede', Ungers claimed, 'there is not one principle, but rather a combination of forms ranging from the single-family house—the larger house and the villa—to the row house. There is the reversal, there is the building complex, and, accordingly, the different ways of living, from an individualistic lifestyle to a collective way of life.' This was denounced as a formalist approach. Looking back, Ungers would say, 'At Team 10 it was difficult to present because they were only looking at the social aspect. Aldo van Eyck and Giancarlo de Carlo only recognised the principle of social distress and its alleviation. Architecture cannot—and this I tried to make clear to them, and that was also the breach—solve social problems. It is incapable of doing so.'[2]

The next Team 10 meeting in 1966 was organised by Giancarlo de Carlo and took place in the newly finished Collegio del Colle. The Smithsons famously did not attend. The differences among the group sparked a crisis, and the future of Team 10 was put into question. In his statement after the meeting, De Carlo concluded that if they were to move on, they would have to assess what kept them together, and 'face their ideological background: the moral, political,

2 Rem Koolhaas, Hans-Ulrich Obrist, 'An Interview with O.M. Ungers', *Log*, no. 16 (Spring/Summer 2009), 50–95.

rational, utopian pattern from which we derive both theoretical lines and architectural forms'. A few months after Ungers returned from Urbino, he published a pamphlet manifesto, *Grossformen im Wohnungsbau,* addressing the 'greater number' at an urban scale. To illustrate his argument on the 'large form', an attempt to discern formally coherent urban figures as building blocks for the city, he compiled a set of examples, including the work of Le Corbusier, the Smithsons and the Torre Velasca. Architecture cannot solve social problems. It cannot shape entire lives. It can only make singular, formally coherent places as containers for life to unfold. Ungers was not invited to the next Team 10 meeting, which focused on participation and open design. Later, Van Eyck would write a 'Letter to Mathias Ungers from another world', denouncing him for being totally at odds with everything that Team 10 stood for. The diverse group, loosely united by a shared opposition to the legacy of their forebears, was forever burdened by the responsibility of succession. While denouncing any trace of authoritarian repression, they remained trapped in cryptic generalities and were ultimately undone by their own good intentions.

When in 1968 protesters besieged the opening of the XIV Milan Triennale organised by

Giancarlo de Carlo, he decided to face the crowd and hear their demands. The serendipity of the event was palpable. The exhibition was devoted to the theme of 'Il Grande Numero', and after a last-minute decision of the US to withdraw its participation, De Carlo had solved the problem of the empty space with an installation titled 'Protest of the Youth', a homage to the ongoing civil unrest in Paris. The room was lined with photo panels of the protests and adorned with rubble and paving stones, along with a barricade made of junk home appliances, complete with an overturned car. Leading lights of Team 10—Van Eyck, the Smithsons, Bakema, Candilis and Woods—as well as Archigram, were invited to exhibit their work in what was supposed to be an ethical examination of the profound impact of the population explosion and consumerism on a rapidly changing industrial society. The Parisian riot scenography, like the rest of the Triennale, would not only show cutting-edge consumer products (like the previous edition, which had focused on leisure and free time), but would enact *environments*, transforming visitors into participants. So absorbed was De Carlo in his efforts to simulate reality—to directly convert political and utopian patterns into architectural form—that he somehow failed to register the magnitude of the real events taking shape outside. During the official opening ceremony and press conference, while men in suits were speechifying on a podium in front of the Palazzo dell'Arte building, around one hundred artists and students of art and architecture gathered in a protest organised by the Association of Painters and Sculptors of Milan. For the demonstrators, it did not matter what the exhibition was about. It was 30 May 1968 and the event had the potency of a global meaning: *Against Institution. Alienation of Intellectual Work. Commodification of Culture.* After a brief altercation with the police, the protesters were allowed to enter the building, to avoid further incident. Once inside, they declared the Triennale 'occupied' and promptly vandalised the exhibits. It would be a week before they were evicted, and another month before the damage was repaired and the exhibition reopened. But the point had already been made. What could be seen as the last Team 10 outing ended in failure, eaten by their own public.

In the midst of these events, another commission came from the University of Urbino, but this time the site was in the old town. It had once housed a convent and a small adjacent church, but the only structure still standing was a perimeter brick wall. There was no space here to develop a theory, no pattern that could grow, no place for any moral or political conviction (which must have been a relief, after Milan). The Faculty of Education (Il Magistero) was to accommodate 1,500 students, and the building could only expand inwards, into the hill. This was an exercise in the densification and distortion of ideal units. A 16m-deep pit was excavated to contain the six-storey building. The operation was that of carving out: a circular courtyard and a semicircular glazed amphitheatre were extracted from the mass, and all the rooms arranged within the residual space. Here De Carlo's affinity with Francesco di Giorgio was not only conceptual, but a matter of practicality and form.

The forced excavation of the Magistero involved a number of design techniques that are superficially aligned with Team 10 themes, but are in fact radically different. Space is defined by figures and voids with different scales and presence. Space is organised through an array of urban furniture that mediates between void and mass. Sameness (of type, unit, experience) is replaced by an emphasis on radical contrasts: light and dark, big and small, full and empty. The depth of the site is embraced as an opportunity (not a problem) and understood as the *thickness* of the project. An array of fitted furniture pieces allows the user to *experience* and traverse the thick building. As the only devices that cut through its three dimensions—joining, bridging, connecting the different spatial experiences—they create the environment. Fixed furniture becomes both guide and protagonist. Architecture is a container of various spatial experiences, a fortress, a collection of inverted urban figures: a *large form*.

All the projects De Carlo built over the next decade attest to this sudden and radical embrace of an encapsulated urbanity. From the 1970s onwards, his experimenting went underground. As the university expanded, additional student housing was required on campus. Large figures make effortless compositions of accumulated units. None of the buildings seem to be particularly extendable, but rather content with their first and final form. Every figure seems finite, fully autonomous from the strange accretions of cells and corridors that appear alongside it. Life was supposed to happen inside, within the strata of these crusty, complex and thick mega-forms that explore the limit of what was architecturally and socially possible: more units, more streets, more squares, more clusters, smaller rooms, longer walkways. The buildings are *rock-like*, thick, turning the existing topography into an artificial one. But while they celebrate thickness and mass, they are still constructed from simple materials—brick walls and concrete lintels. The figures are seemingly designed from the inside, their clumsy exterior the final consequence of some sort of functional formalism. Ultimately, every finite figure uncovers a simple spatial type: roof, labyrinth, stair ... Together, enlarged and inhabited, they present some sort of typological invention. As successive hallucinations of semi-urban utopias, are these buildings testament to an ideological *détournement?*

No more participation, but experimental social condensers. No more differences, but endless repetition. No accumulation of the unit, but semi-autonomous figures. The pattern of growth replaced by menacing thickness. The city buried in the hills of Urbino.

# in Urbino

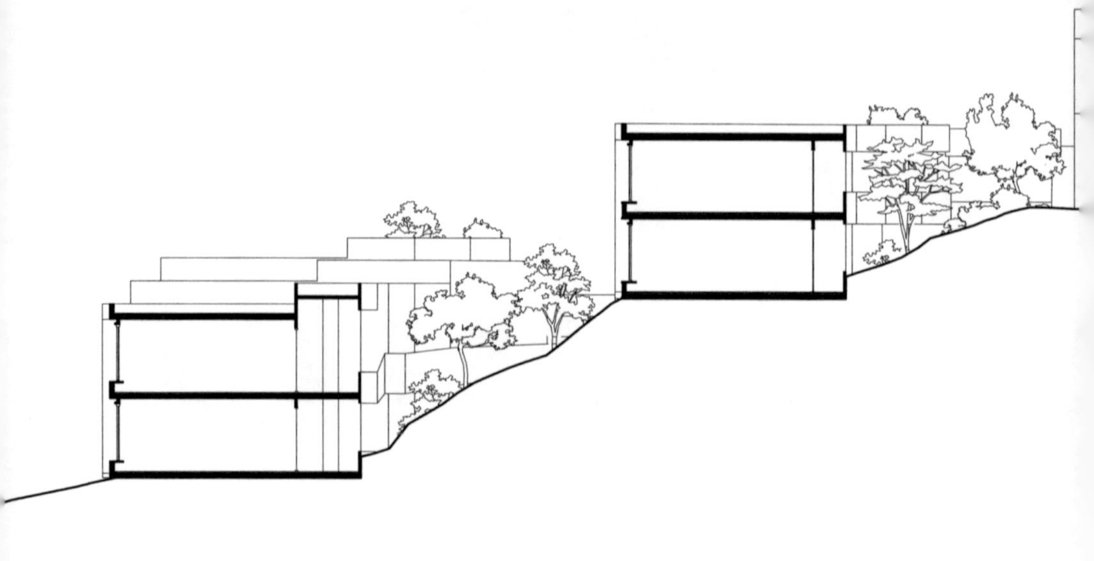

0 1 5m

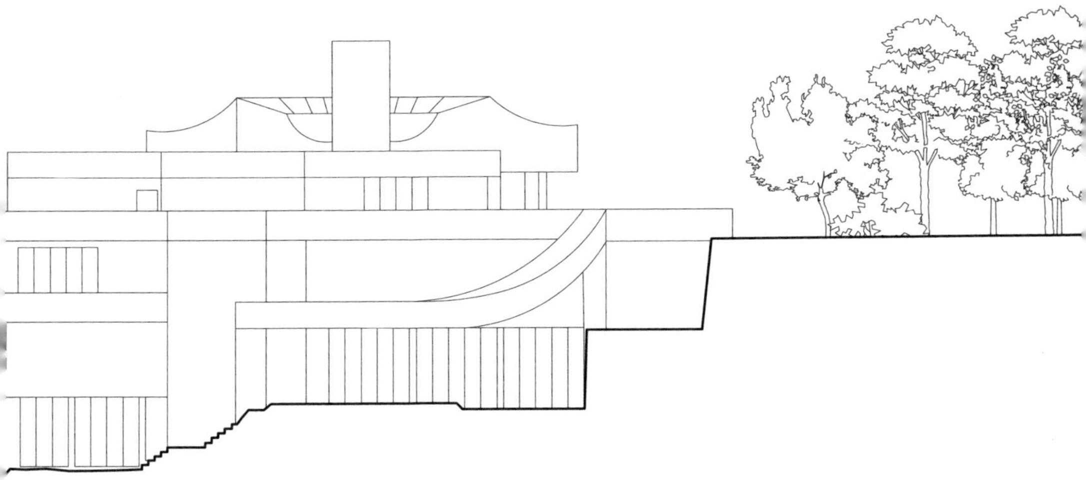

## Faculty of Law 1966–1968

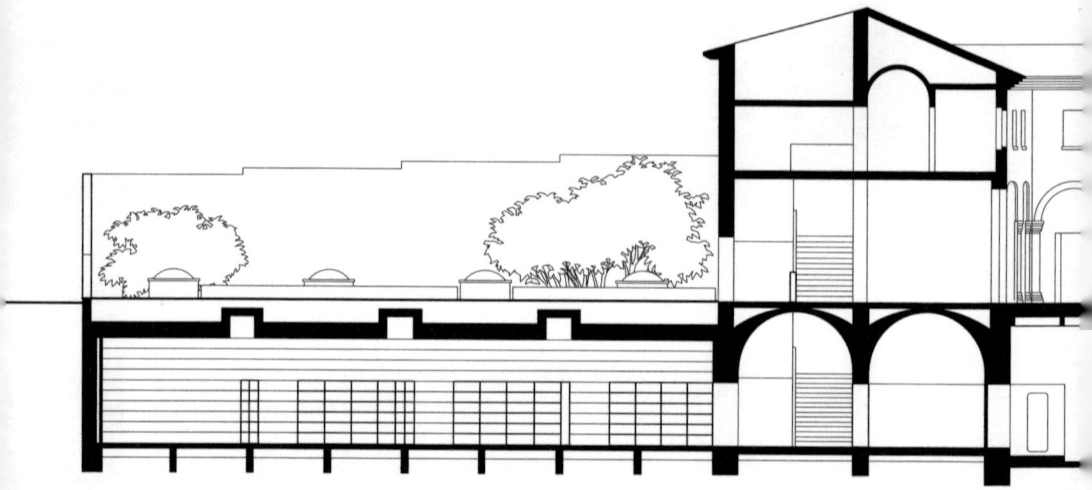

0 1 5m

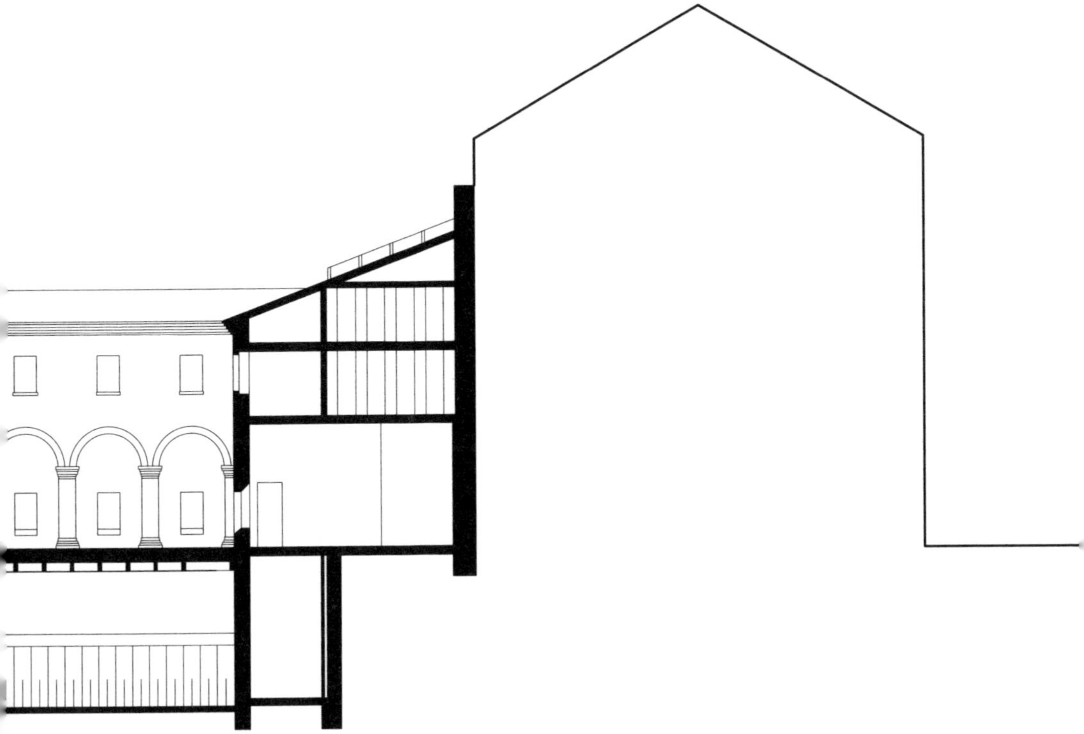

SALA dei PERIODICI

CANONICO
ECCLESIASTICO
DIGESTO
Indici

Un'Europa verde, digitale e inclusiva
entro ed oltre i confini dell'Unione
Guida al diritto
Harvard law review
JUS
Michigan law review

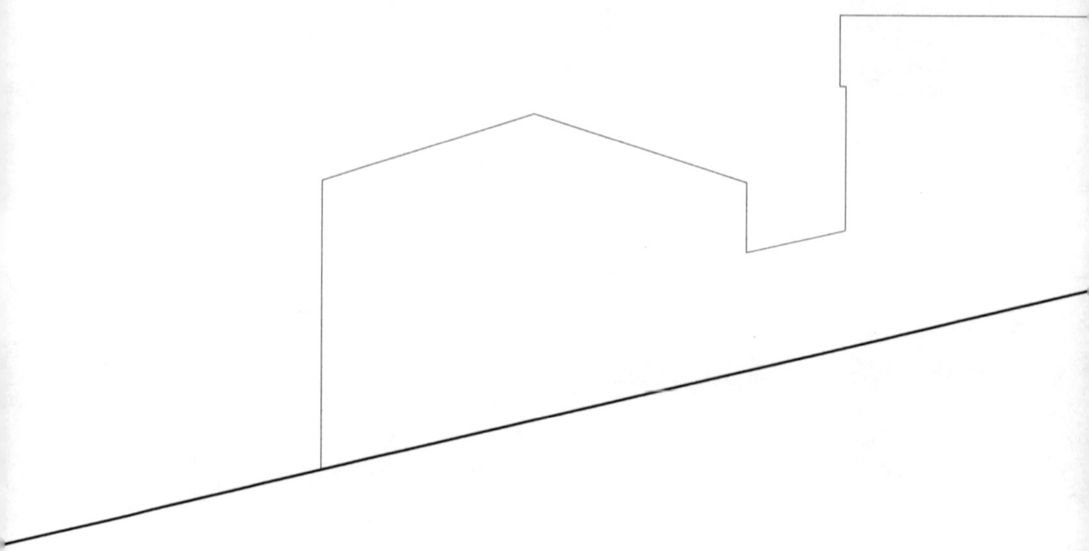

0 1 5m

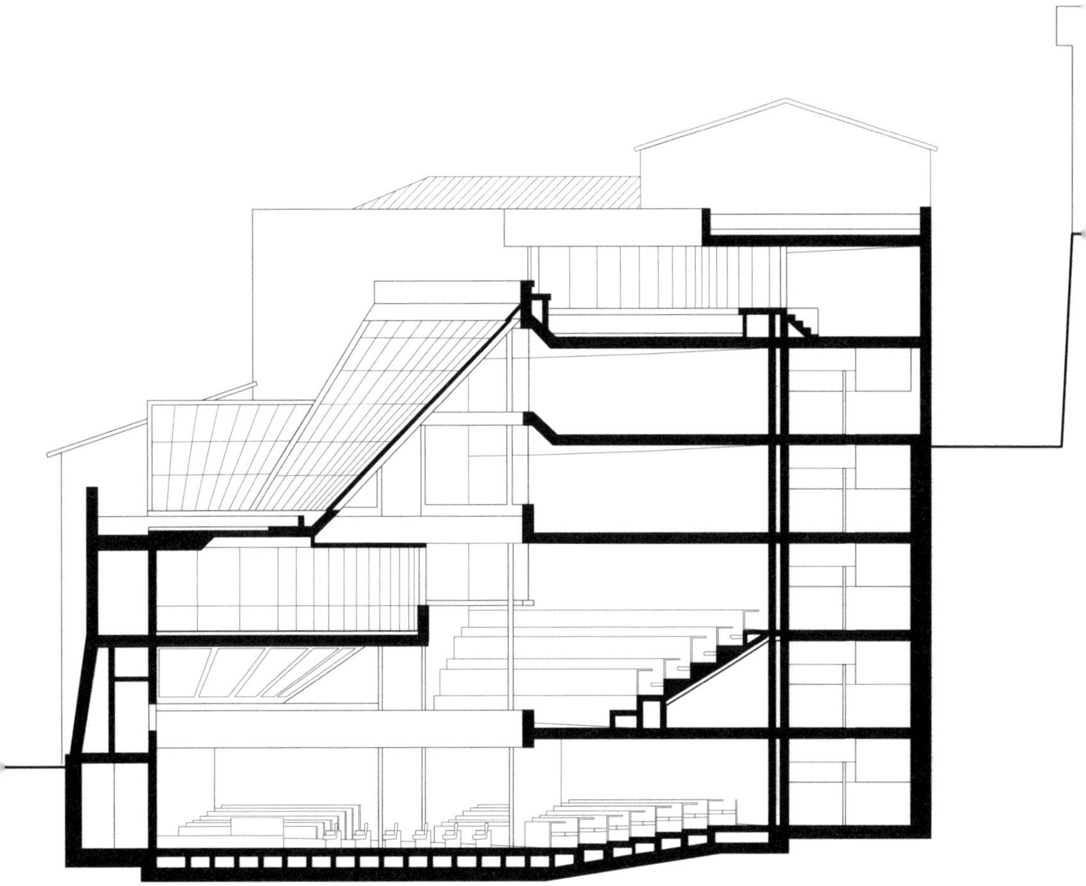

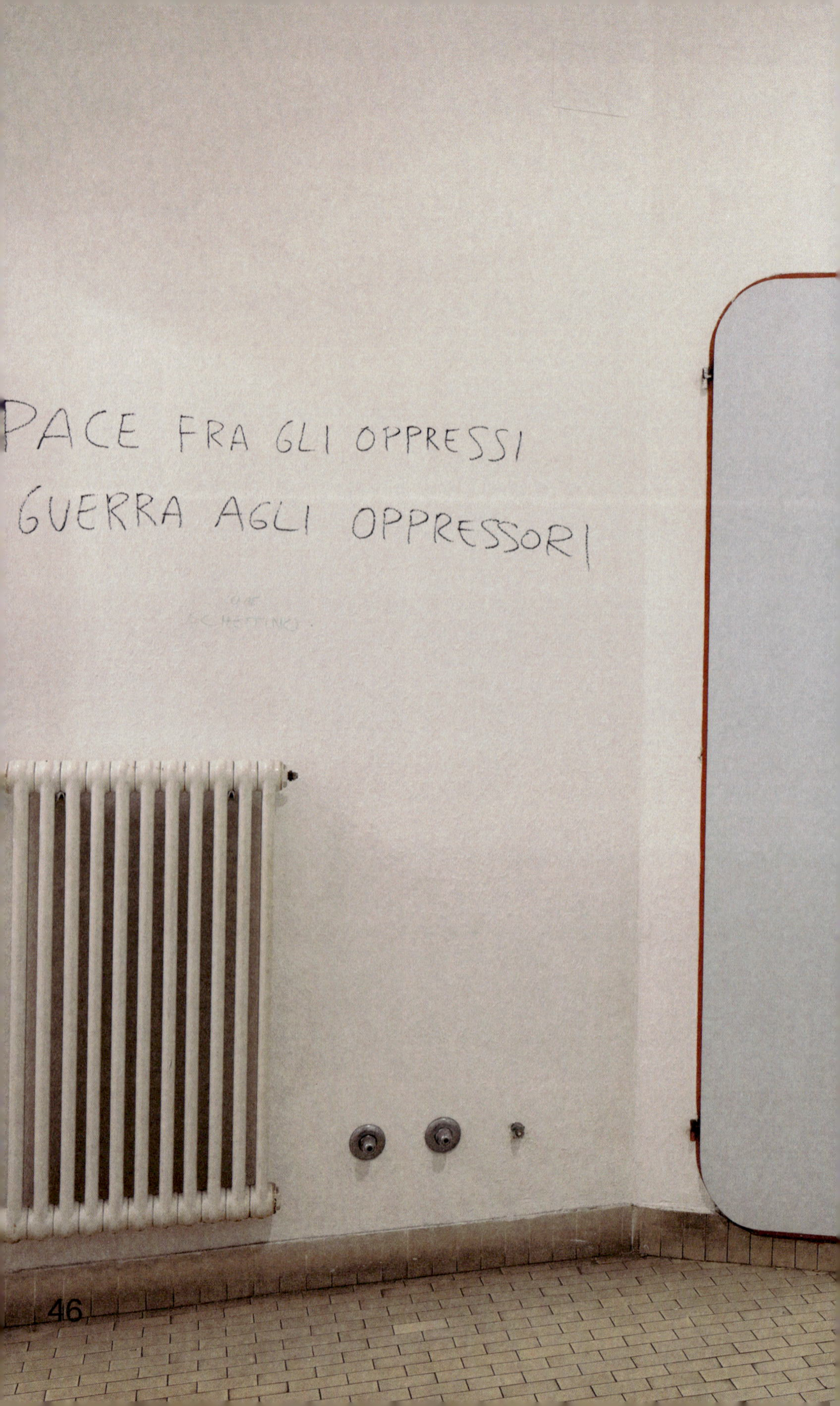
PACE FRA GLI OPPRESSI
GUERRA AGLI OPPRESSORI

URBINO
ANTIFÀ
SARÀ
UNA
GUERRILLA
STICKERS
VI
SEPPELLIRÀ!

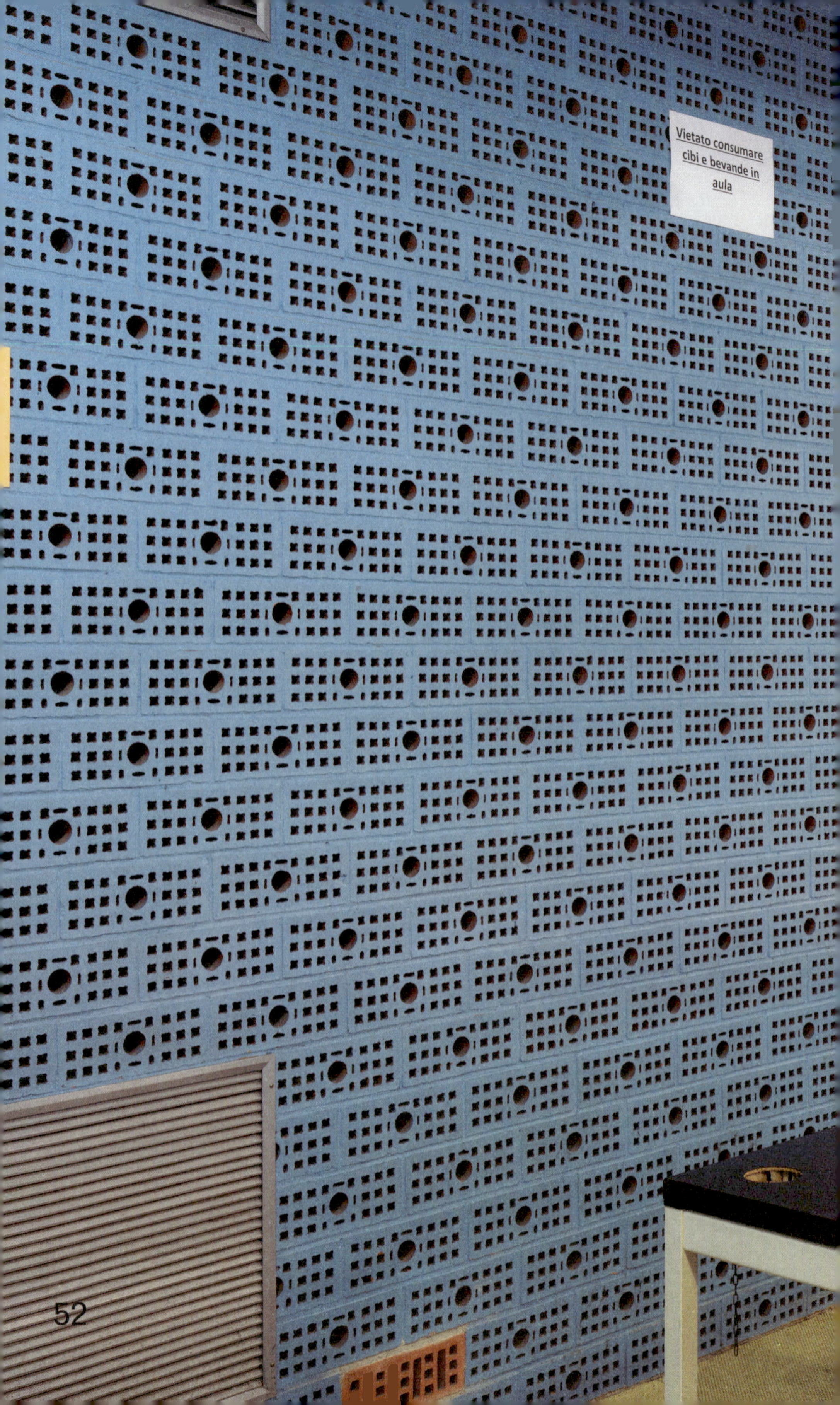
Vietato consumare
cibi e bevande in
aula

Vietato consumare
cibi e bevande in
aula

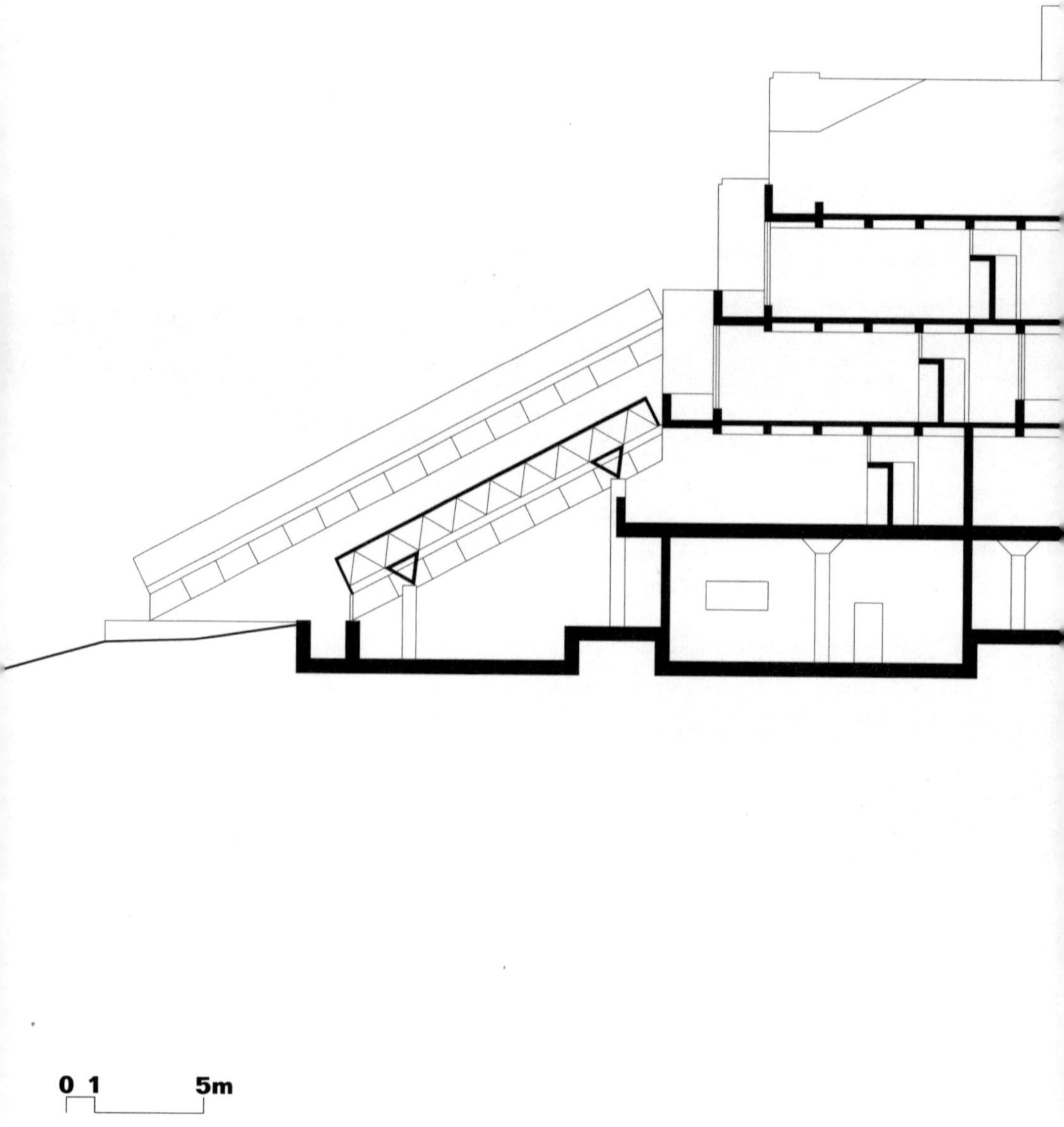

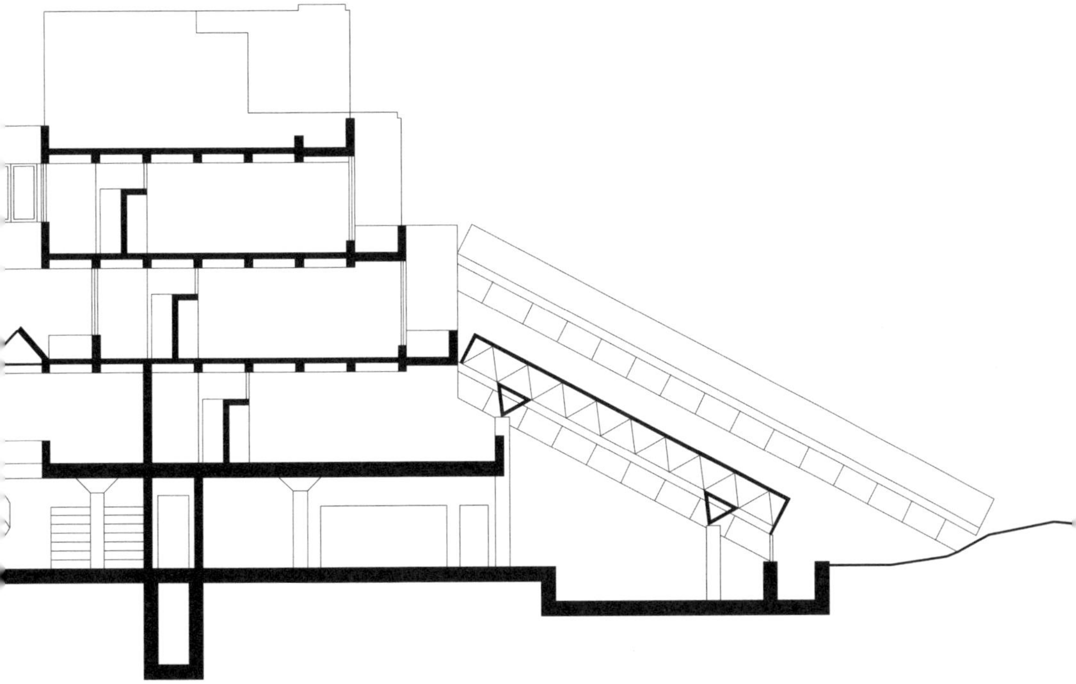

BACK OF THE NECK
SPINE©
BRACCO

Aula
Info2
Design

libro
52

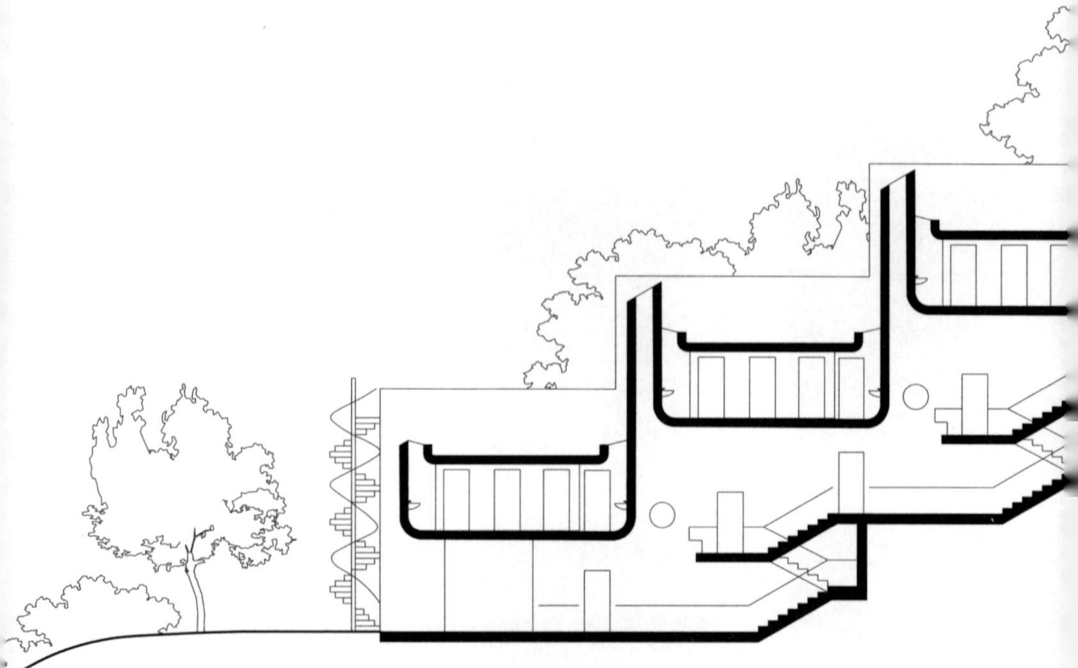
0 1 5m

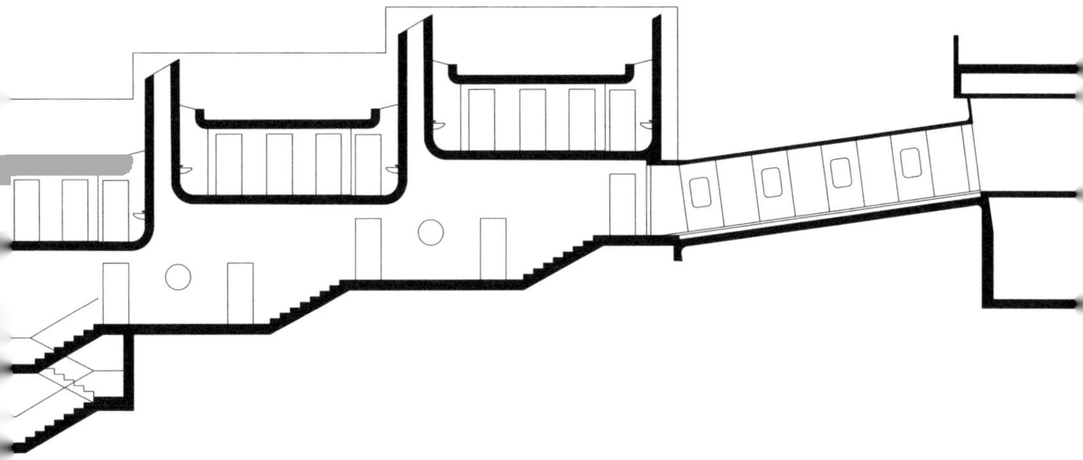

VIETATO
FUMARE

DIVIETO DI FUMO

Segui le indicazioni

DIVIETO DI FUMO

DIVIETO DI FUMO

ATTENZIONE!!!!!!
NON RIMUOVERE I
FILTRI DAL LAVANDINO
E TENERLI PULITI!!!!!!

MP!
2018/19

# Serpentine 1973–1980

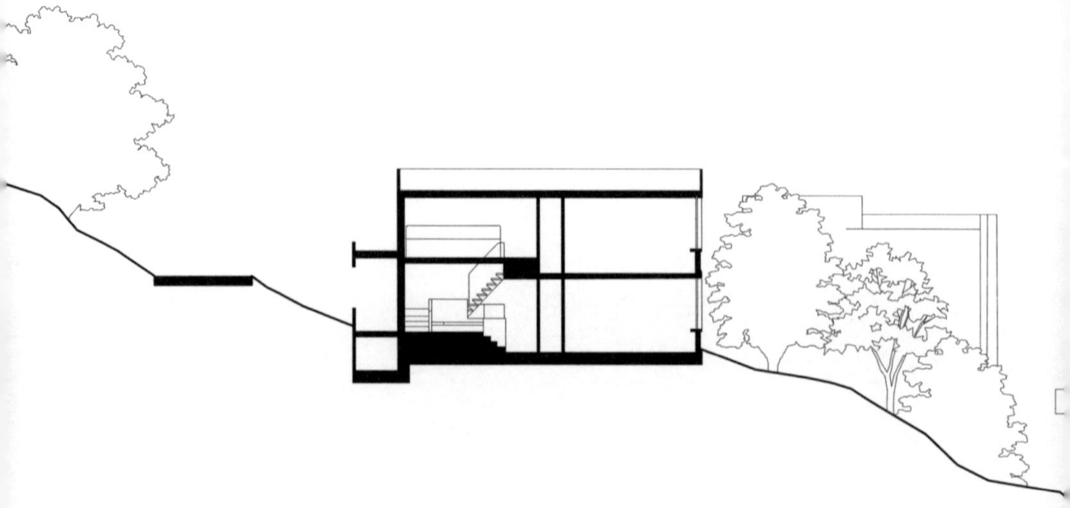

0 1 5m

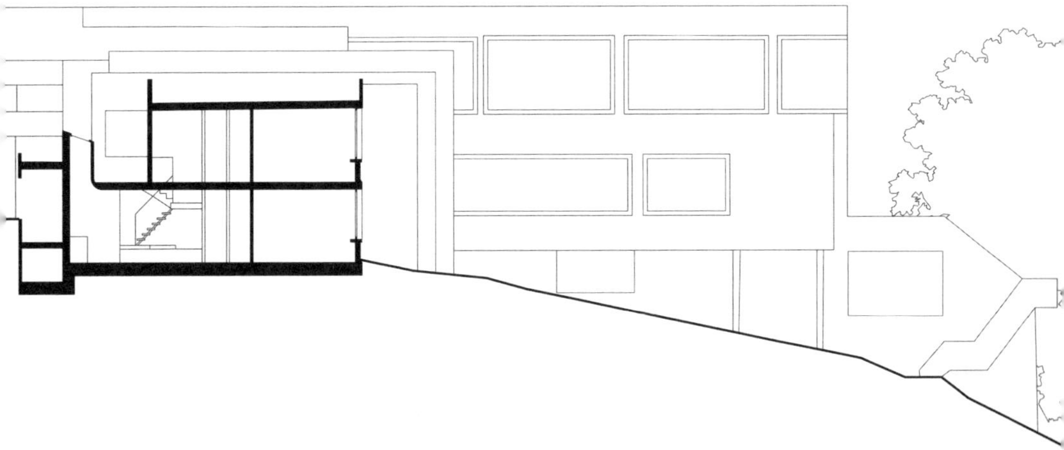

Smetti di
fumare – Vivi
per i tuoi cari

214

stoviglie

## Aquilone 1973–1980

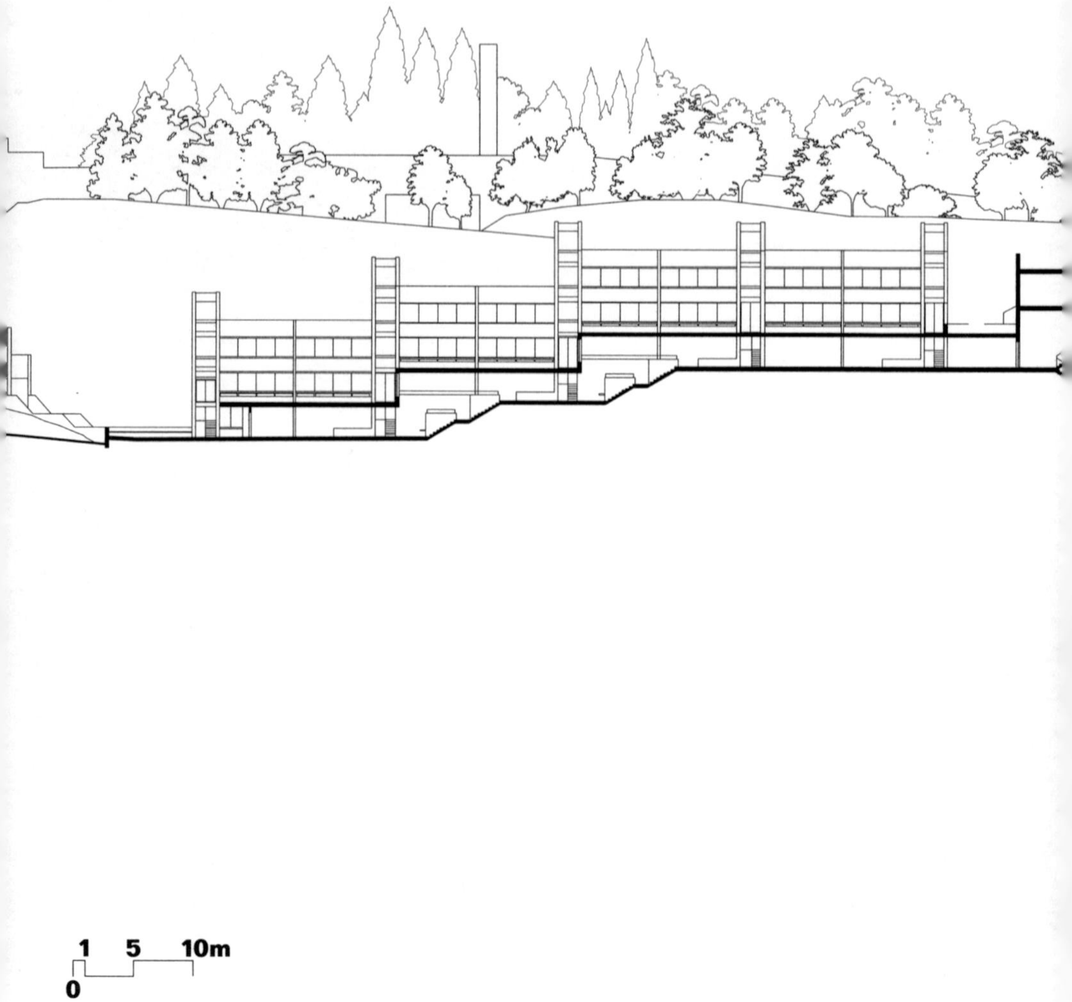

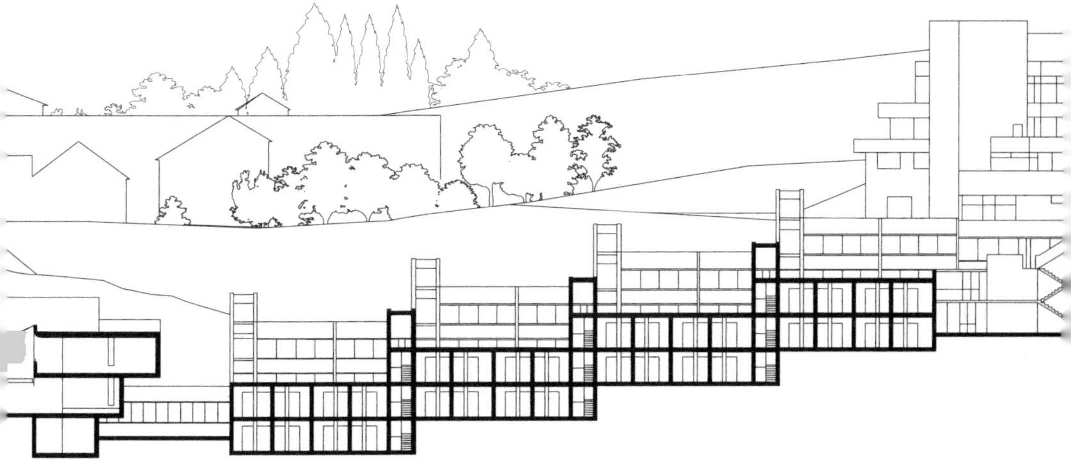

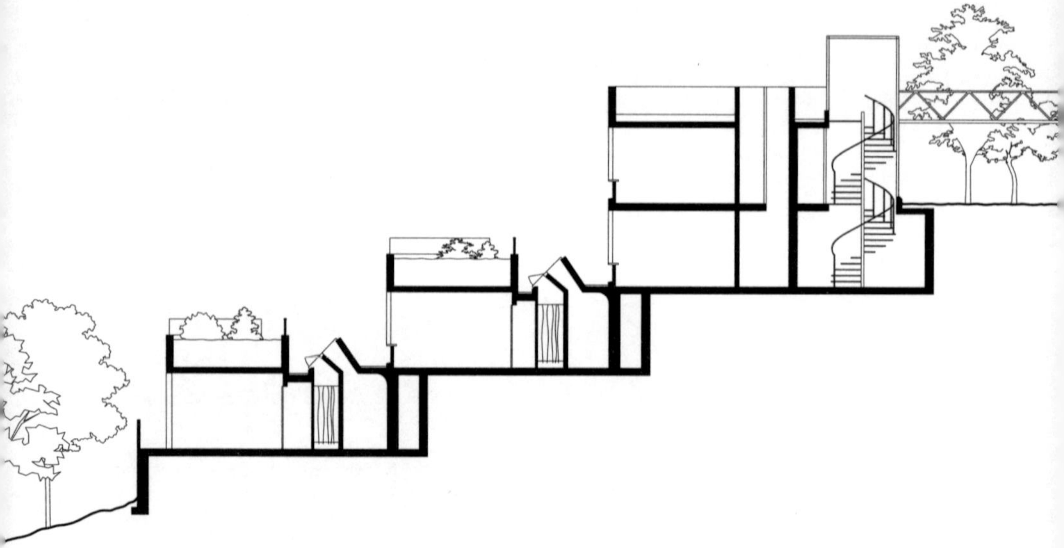

0 1 5m

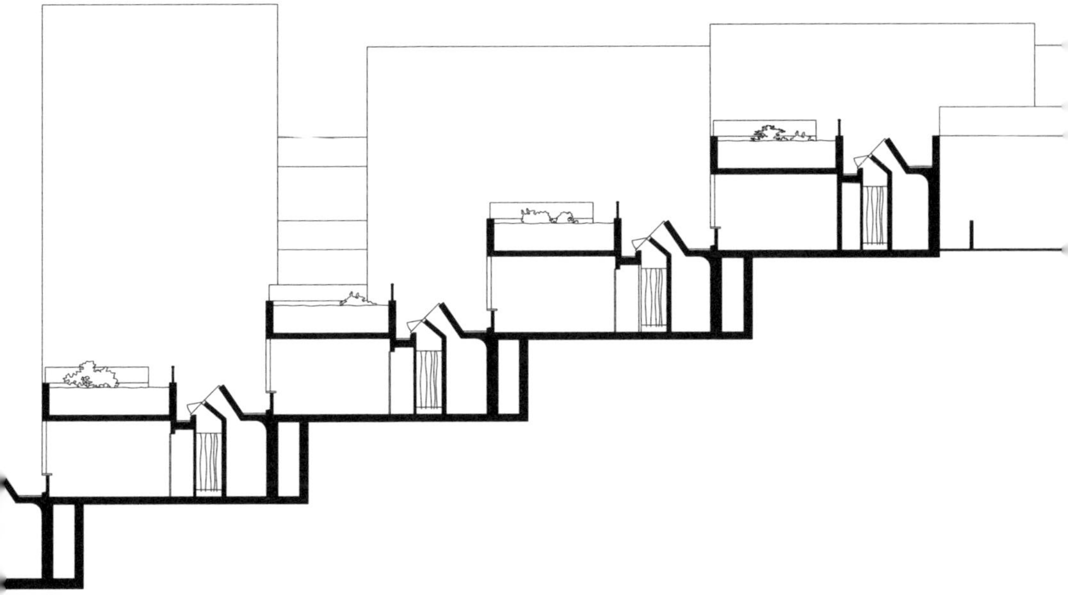

Livello n°2
1-24

Livello n°3 bis
13 - 24

IDRAN
TO BREAK IN CASE
ROMPERE IN CASO D'

Livello n°7
1-24

Sala Studio Liv. N°7

DIVIETO DI FUMO
AULA STUDIO
ORARIO
DALLE ORE 09.00
ALLE ORE 23.00

## Church of San Bernardino

1482–1491

Francesco di Giorgio Martini

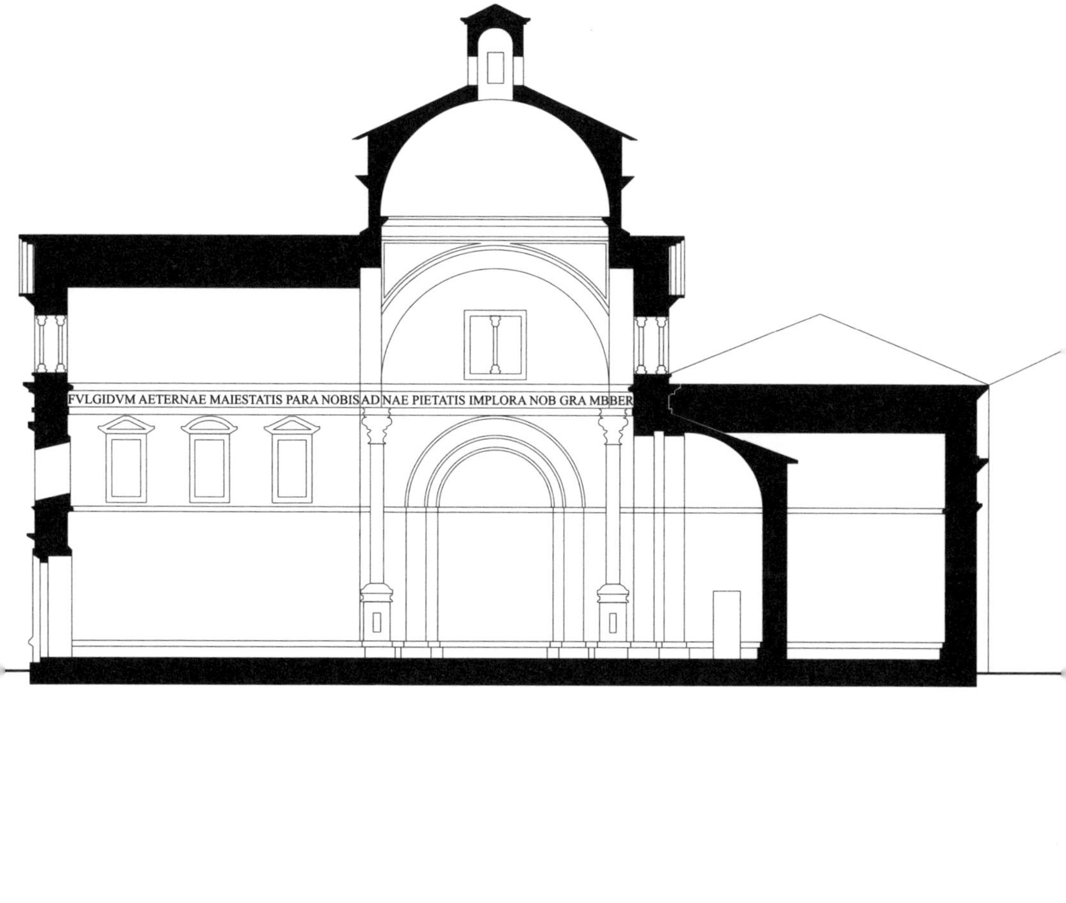
FVLGIDVM AETERNAE MAIESTATIS PARA NOBIS AD NAE PIETATIS IMPLORA NOB GRA MBBER

STRATOR·SAPIENTIÆ·PROTECTOR·VER

ANTE THRONVM

## Giancarlo de Carlo in Urbino



---

## Biography

Giancarlo De Carlo (1919–2005) studied structural engineering at Milan Polytechnic from 1939 to 1943. In Milan in the final years of the war he was active in the Italian Resistance movement, where he met fellow architects Giuseppe Pagano and Franco Albini. From 1948 to 1949 he studied architecture at IUAV Venice. On graduating, he worked for Albini, and set up his own practice in Milan in 1951. From 1953 to 1956 De Carlo was on the editorial staff of *Casabella Continuità*; the magazine's director, Ernesto Nathan Rogers, introduced him to CIAM and he served as a delegate of the Italian group from 1952 until 1960, when CIAM was effectively superseded by Team 10, of which De Carlo was a founding member.

Giancarlo de Carlo first visited Urbino in 1951 when Carlo Bo, rector of the University of Urbino, invited him on the recommendation of the writer (and their mutual friend) Elio Vittorini to carry out a minor refurbishment of his offices. This was the beginning of a complex reorganisation of the university premises that would ultimately grow into a strategy for revitalising the hilltop town, which had been in a steady economic decline since its heyday in the fifteenth and sixteenth centuries. Carlo Bo joined forces with the mayor, Egidio Mascioli, from the Italian Communist Party, to resuscitate the

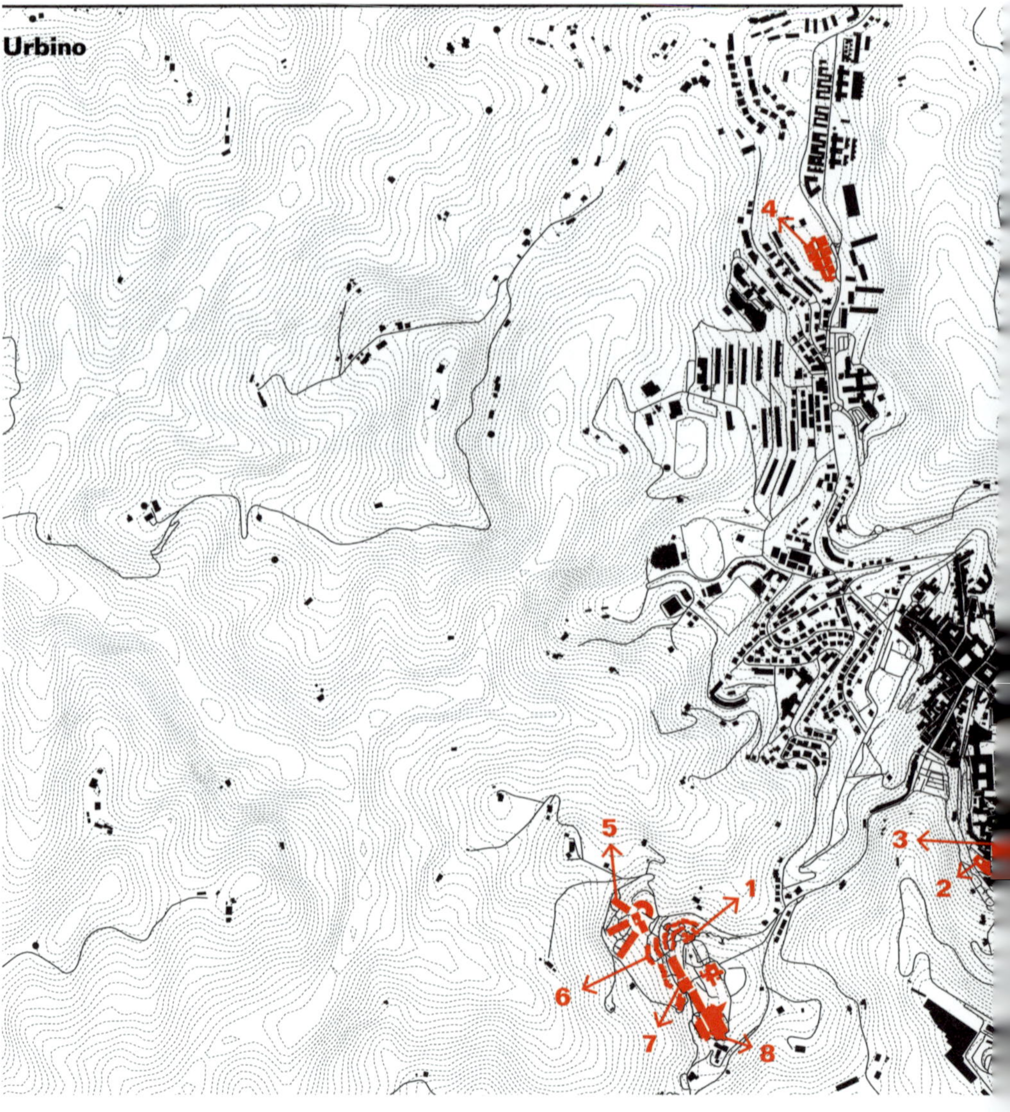

**university, which had been established as early as 1506 by the Duke of Urbino. The two men, who both held long-term posts (the mayor until 1970s and the rector until his death in 2001), secured political and financial support from the state to develop cultural and educational institutions that would reshape the overall urban structure. The expansion and democratisation of higher education in Italy during the postwar boom years resulted in an exponential growth in Urbino's university population, which increased from 139 students in 1939 to around 10,000 in 1966. Giancarlo de Carlo would end up**

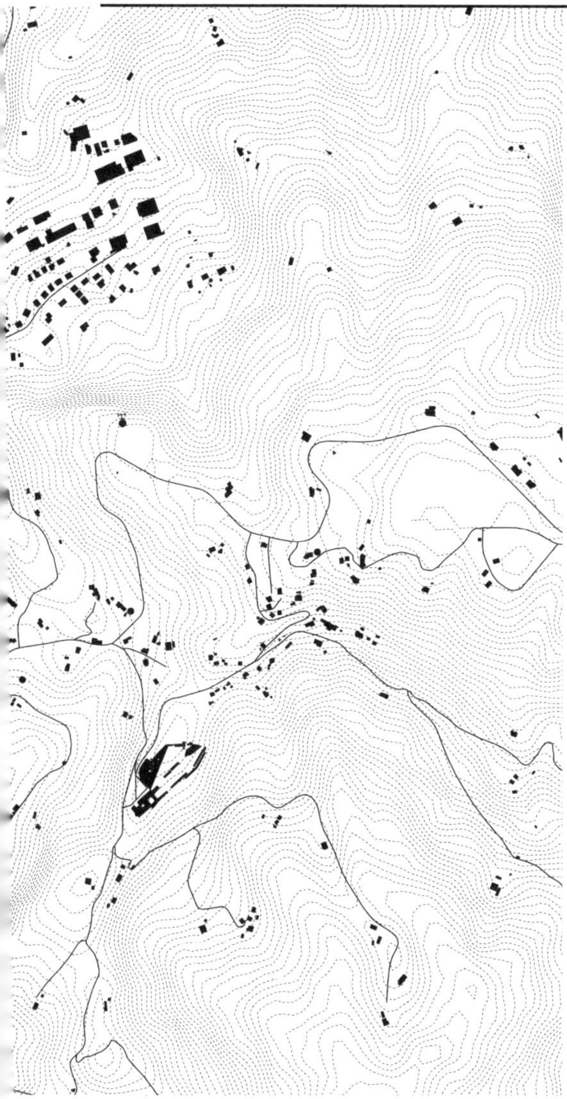

working in Urbino for almost five decades on various projects designed to accommodate this growth. From 1952 to 1954 De Carlo supervised the renovation of the historical Bonaventura Palace to host the university headquarters and the administrative offices. In 1955 he designed housing for university staff—six two-storey buildings with pitched roofs—and between 1958 and 1964 he worked on the masterplan for the conservation of the historical centre and parallel expansion of the university on the slopes of the Colle dei Cappuccini ('hill of the Capuchin friars') 1km beyond the old town, where an entire

---

**1 Colle**

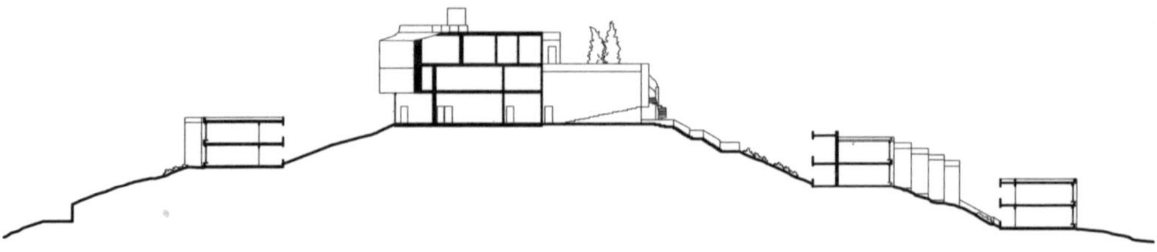

**campus was developed around an existing convent. The collegio del Colle was De Carlo's first major project in Urbino. This first building in the complex, designed in 1960 and built in 1965, is a cluster of student housing, 150 single rooms arranged in two jagged parallel rows that follow the sloping terrain around a central service block. The cluster is subdivided into smaller groups of between 12 and 20 rooms, each arranged over two levels and accessible from interconnected outdoor paths. Whereas the rooms are rather stark, with a private bathroom and bed and desk as the only furniture, the four-level**

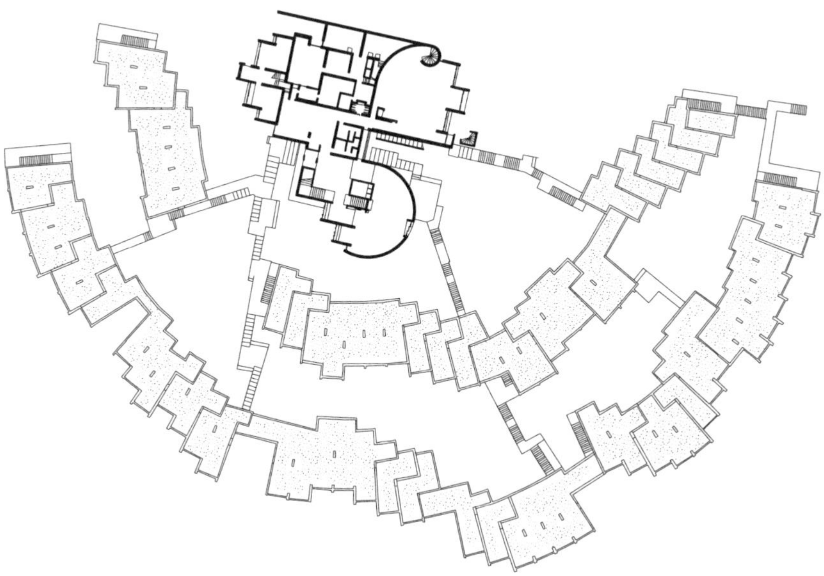

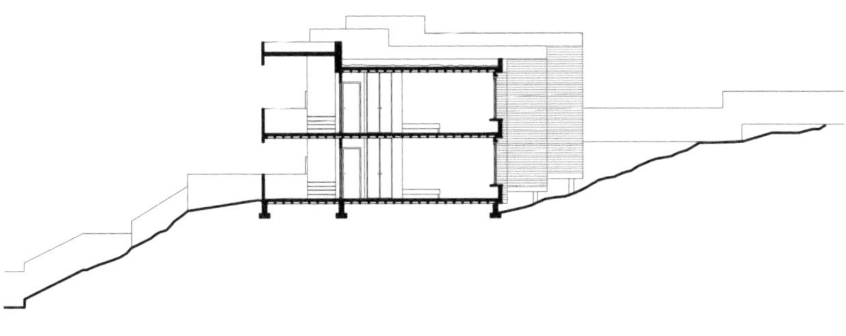

**service centre provides generous common spaces: lounges, study areas, a canteen with a kitchen, a conference room, offices and technical spaces. The building has a unique materiality throughout the interior and exterior: a combination of exposed loadbearing red brick and cast concrete, with interior walls occasionally plastered, and wooden doors and window frames painted white. The flat roofs are not accessible. With the issue of student housing (seemingly) resolved, the university turned its attention to expanding teaching facilities, buying property in the old town for adaptive reuse. In 1966**

---

**2 Faculty of Law**

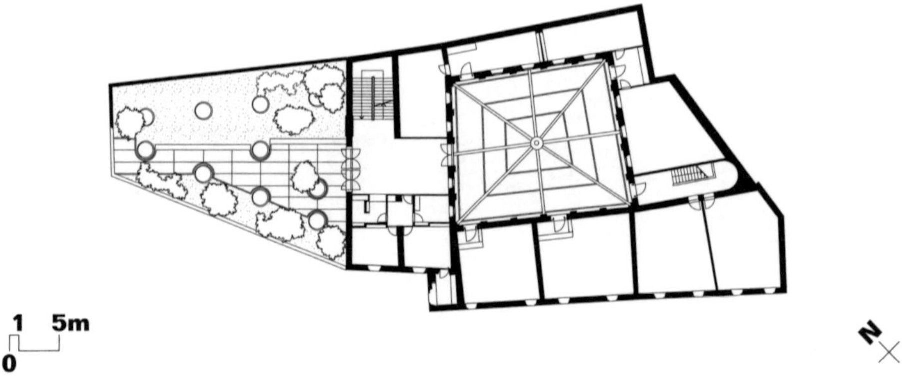


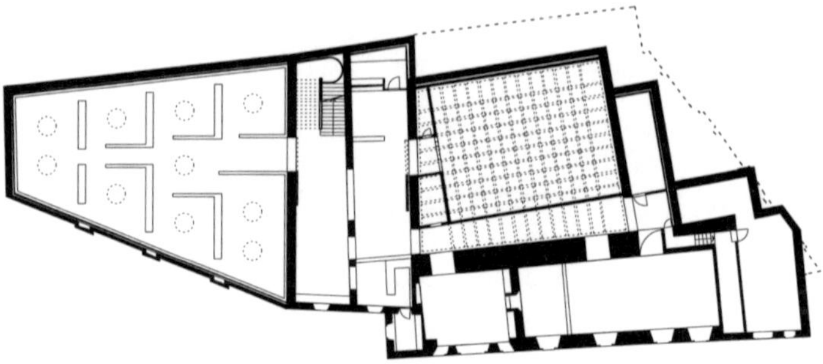

**De Carlo started work on the Faculty of Law, which was finished two years later. It was housed in the former Sant'Agostino convent, built in the eighteenth century, but converted into an orphanage by the mid-nineteenth century. The building had a two-storey rectilinear cloister with a central courtyard and an adjacent garden. De Carlo demolished redundant internal walls to make classrooms accessible from the inner courtyard, and organised the entrance area with administrative offices and a new staircase in the wing facing the garden. His major intervention, however, was not the reconstruction of the building**

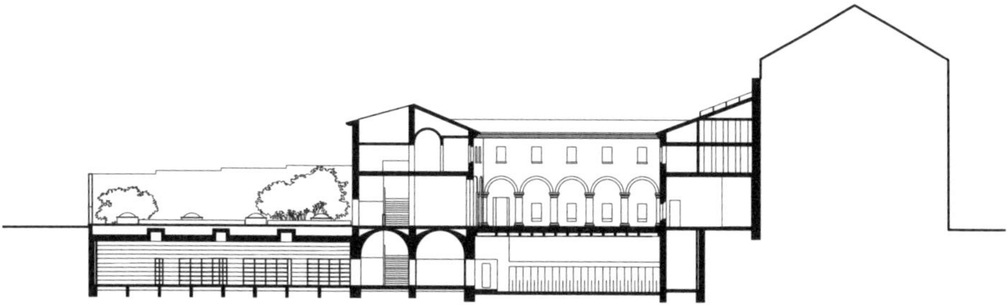

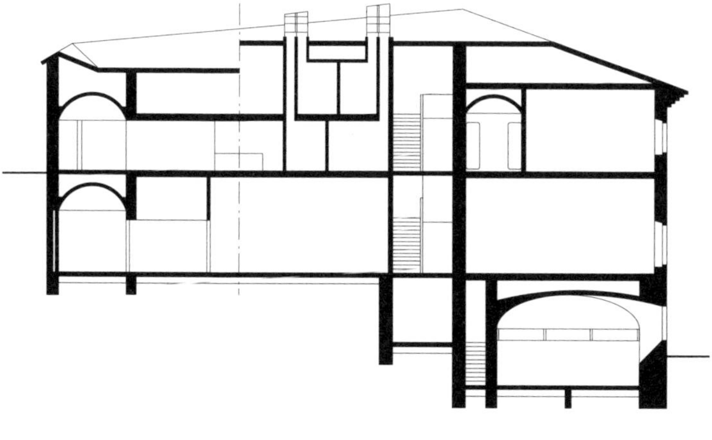

itself, but the excavation of the front garden and the area under the central courtyard to accommodate a library and adjacent book stacks. The garden was populated with ten glass domes—skylights for the underground library. Existing cellars with vaulted brick ceilings were integrated into the newly hollowed out space. A bunker-like sensation was enhanced with rounded doors and portholes. De Carlo would expand this operation in his subsequent project for the Magistero, or Faculty of Education, which he started in 1968, the same year the Faculty of Law was completed. This time, the site contained the

---

**3 Magistero**

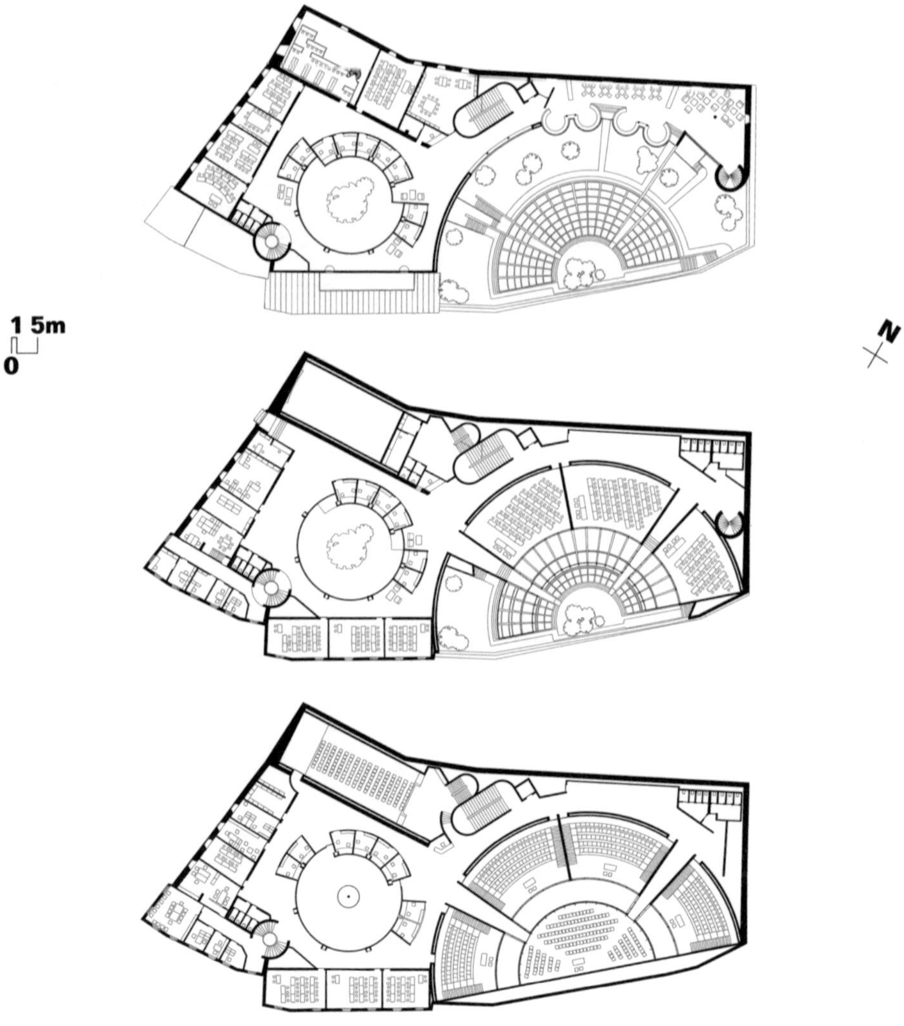

larger eighteenth-century convent of Santa Maria della Bella, but the original building enclosed within massive perimeter brick walls was in a state of complete ruin, and only the adjacent small church in the corner of the plot was worth renovating. De Carlo kept the existing perimeter walls and dug a 16m-deep pit below the garden, into which he inserted a six-storey building. Two main voids were then carved out of this volume: a circular courtyard partly surrounded by faculty offices, and a semicircular amphitheatre ringed with lecture halls, all lit from above by a massive fan of glass. These lecture halls

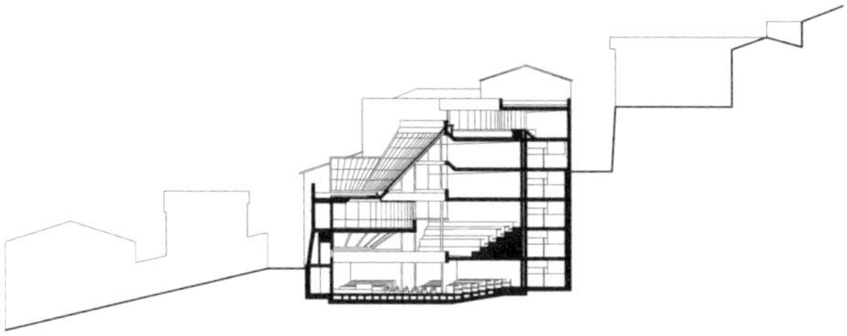

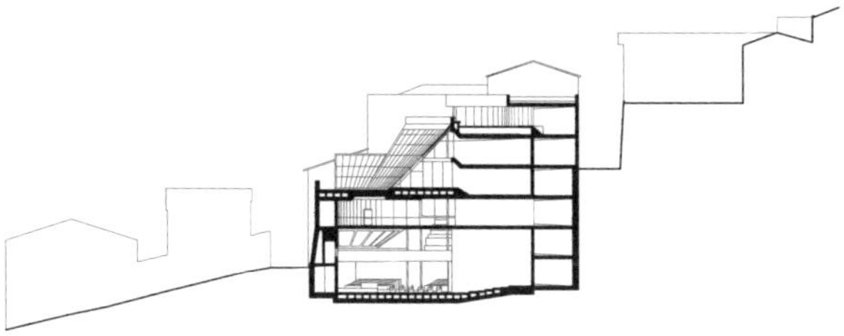

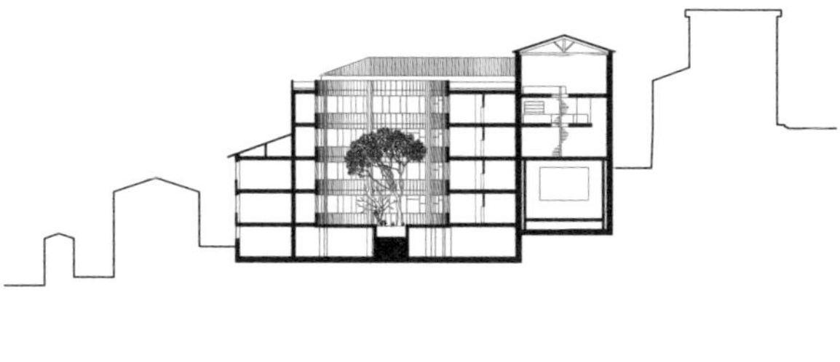

span four floors and can merge into a single *aula magna* seating up to 1,500 people. All the classrooms, technical rooms and staircases are arranged in the remaining space along the perimeter. The larger rooms—an experimental cinema accessible from the street, a library and a meeting room—are placed below and within the volume of the former church, which was likewise hollowed out. While the circular courtyard, with its planting of trees, is not accessible, the inverted glass cone encases a multilevel roof garden. De Carlo later worked on other educational facilities in Urbino, most of them smaller

**4 Scuola del Libro**

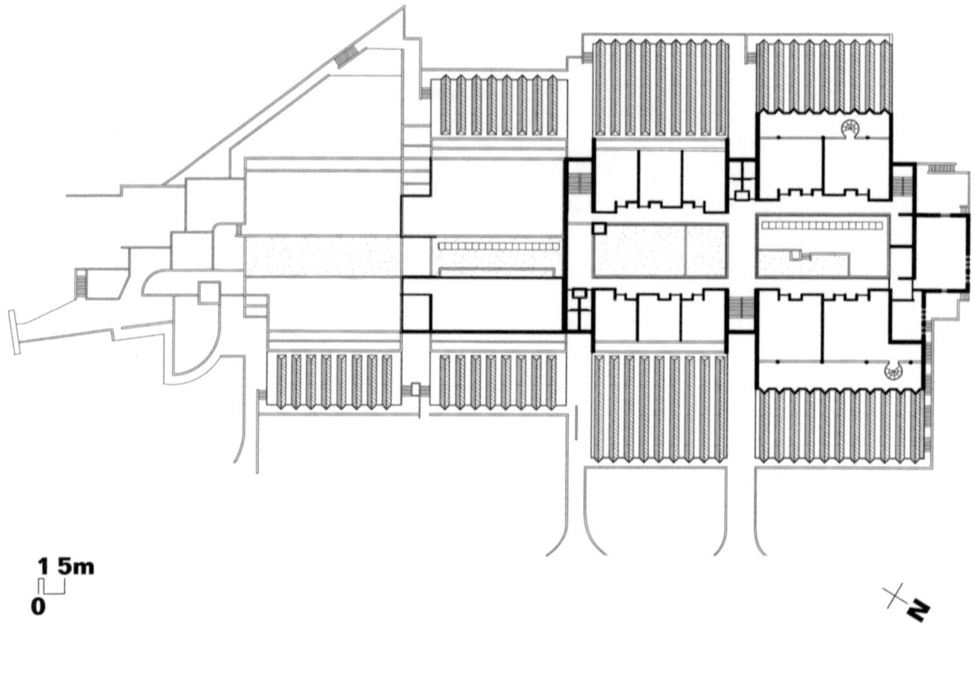


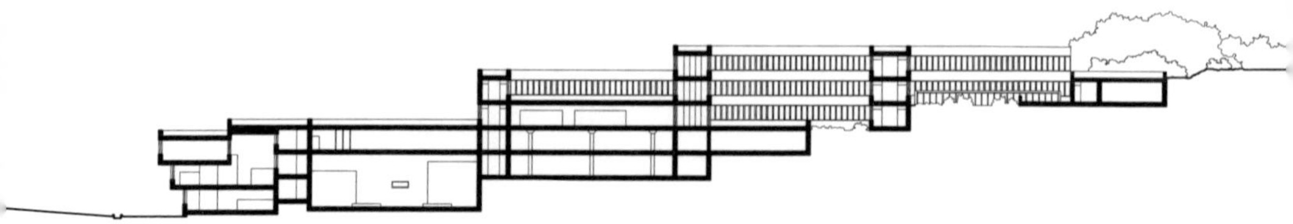

interventions in the historical palazzi. The one notable exception is the Scuola del Libro ('book school') built in 1983, across the street from La Pineta, a group of three massive residential blocks designed by De Carlo in the 1960s in a densely populated area 2km north of the old town. De Carlo's masterplan envisaged these *grand ensembles* as the northern gate of the city, embedded in the hill and so integrated into the Urbino landscape. The housing complex and, later, the book school—relocated here from the Ducal Palace, and famed for its tradition of illustrated manuscripts—were supposed to curb

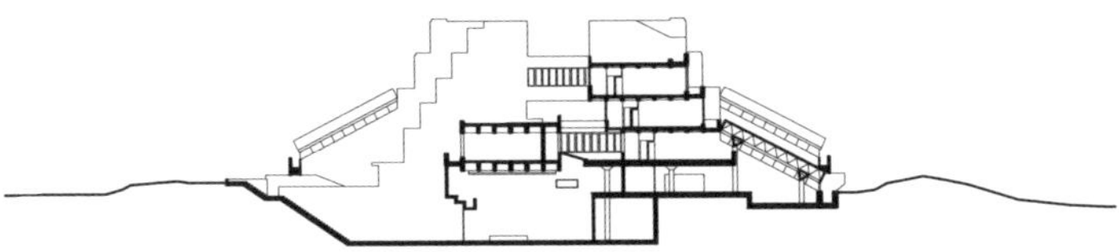

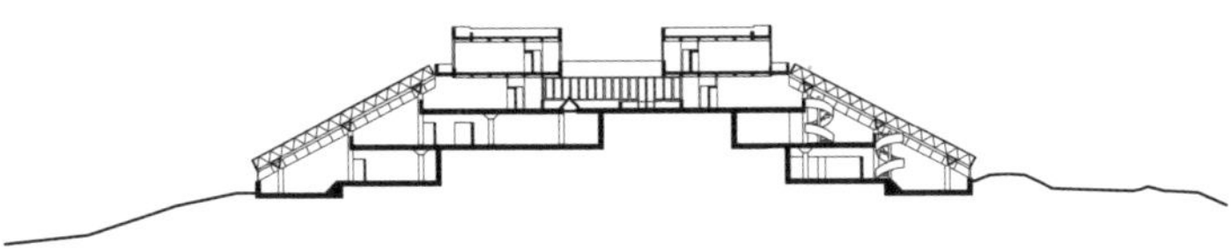

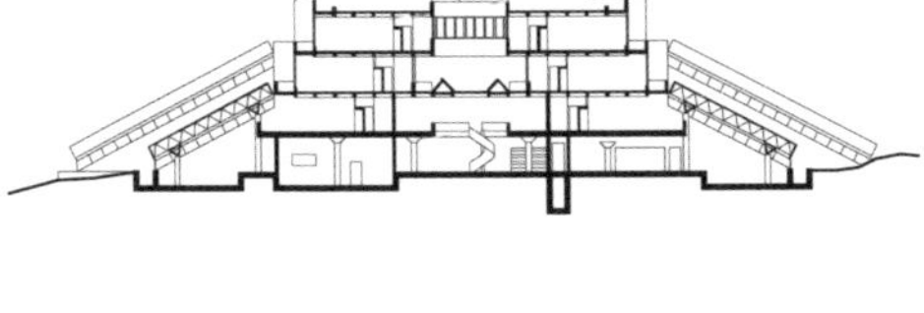

the unregulated postwar housing development, establishing the point beyond which the city should not expand. In the end, only part of the scheme for the book school would be built, and this aspect remains difficult to perceive. The building should have extended symmetrically, doubling its current length. Cut along its projected central axis, the built half has a truncated pyramid section with an open ground floor for the common workshop—today interrupted by a wall—and smaller ateliers on the upper galleries. Outside, the site of the unbuilt portion of the building is used as a parking lot.

## 5 Tridente

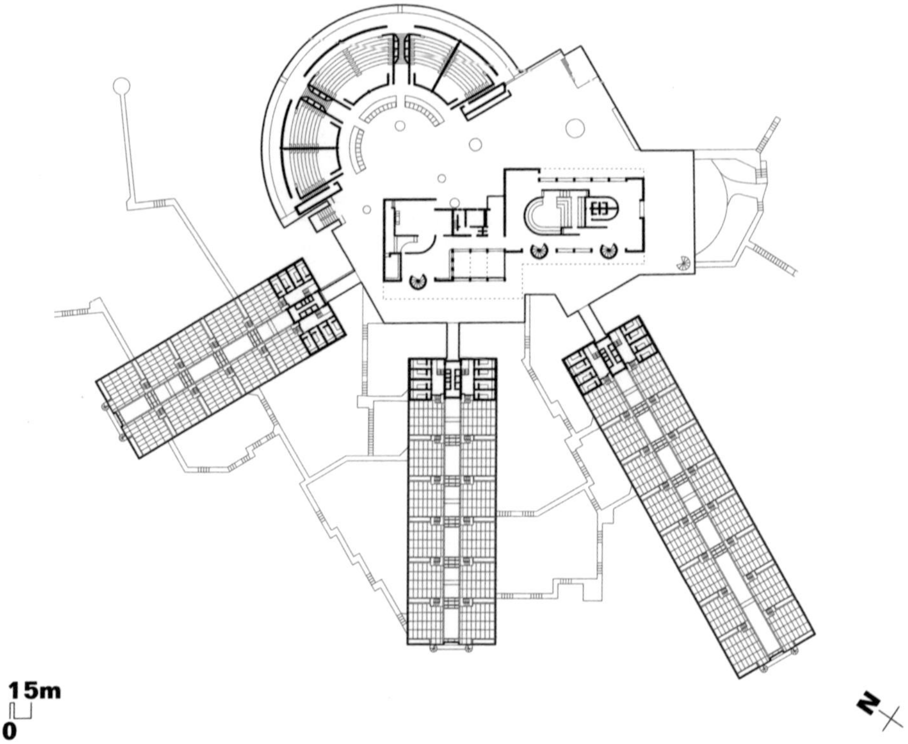


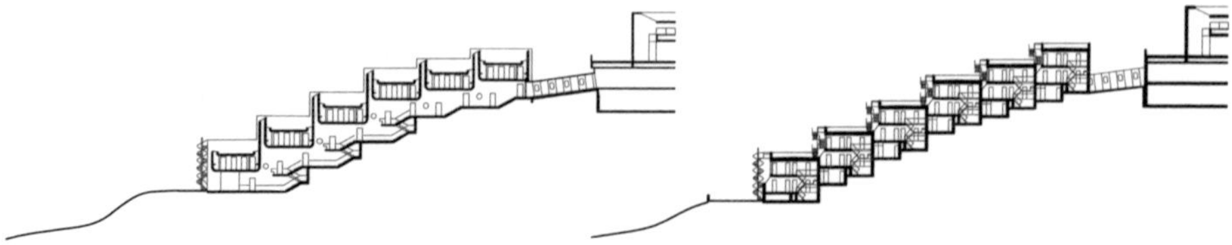

**If De Carlo did not succeed in imposing order on the growth of the new town, which soon extended beyond the limits of the Scuola del Libro, he was still able to completely control the development of the university campus. A few years after the completion of the Collegio del Colle, the university again faced a housing shortage. This time De Carlo was commissioned to develop halls of residence for around 1,000 students, a tenfold increase on the existing capacity. His idea was to simulate an organic city growth. The 'Nuovi Collegi', as they are commonly known, were built between 1973 and 1980. Given the many**

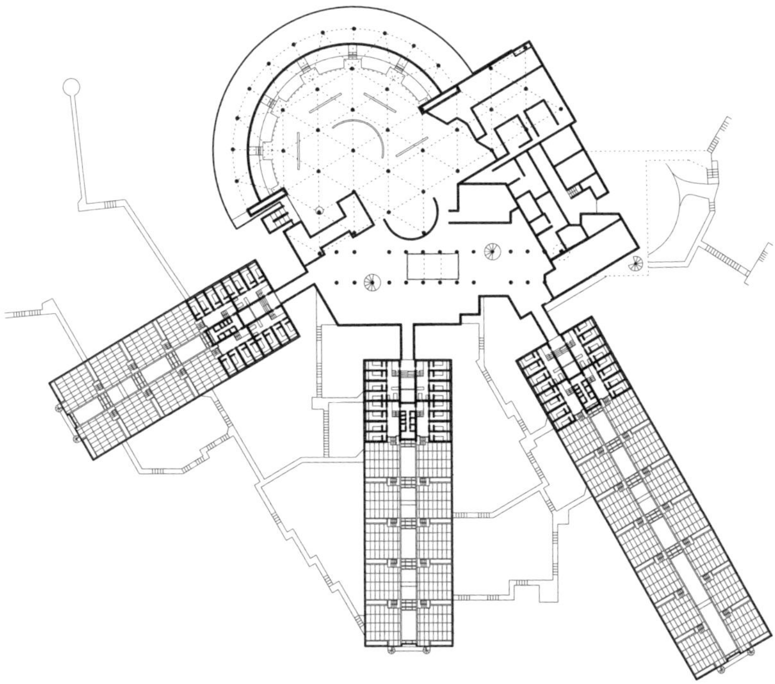

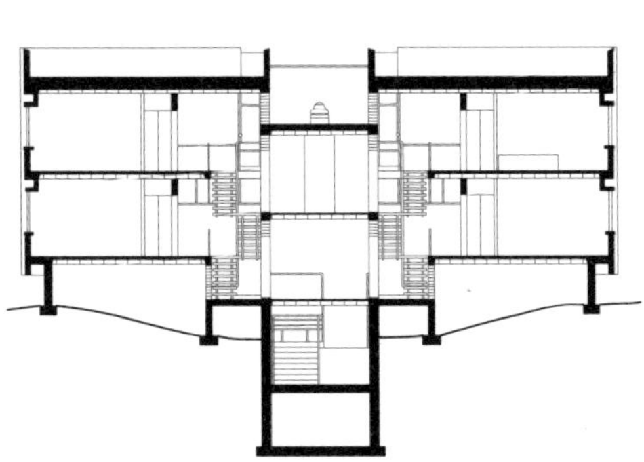

**constraints and consecutive land acquisition, the complex extension was planned in three phases: Block A (today known as 'Vela'), Block B ('Tridente') and Block C ('Aquilone' and 'Serpentine'). The first building to be realised was Tridente, with 352 single rooms distributed over three 'arms' that follow the slope of the land. Each of the arms has an identical layout, with the accommodation arranged symmetrically over two storeys either side of an internal street. Each 16-room cluster has a small common area with a kitchenette and a dining table as well as a shared bathroom, which is placed in the centre**

---

**6 Serpentine**

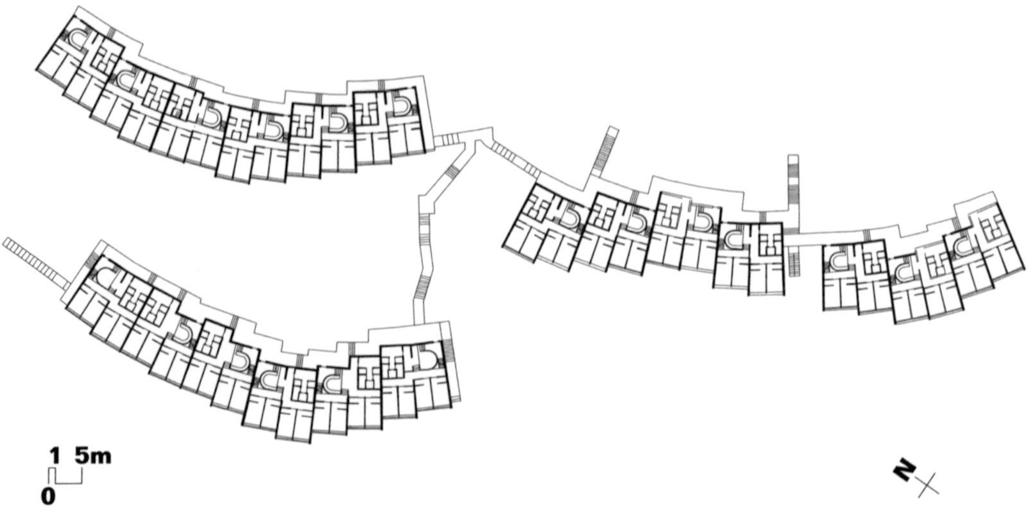

**of the building, above the corridor, and illuminated by narrow skylights. All the rooms have access to the roof terraces. The three arms are connected by tubular corridors to the central service building with the common areas, study rooms, a canteen with a kitchen, and a parking lot, which is partly sunken to form a public square with a semicircular auditorium. To achieve a visual consistency with the Collegio del Colle, all the new buildings on the campus share the same materiality of exposed brick and concrete. Interior furnishings and metal rails are painted red, blue or white throughout the complex to mark areas**

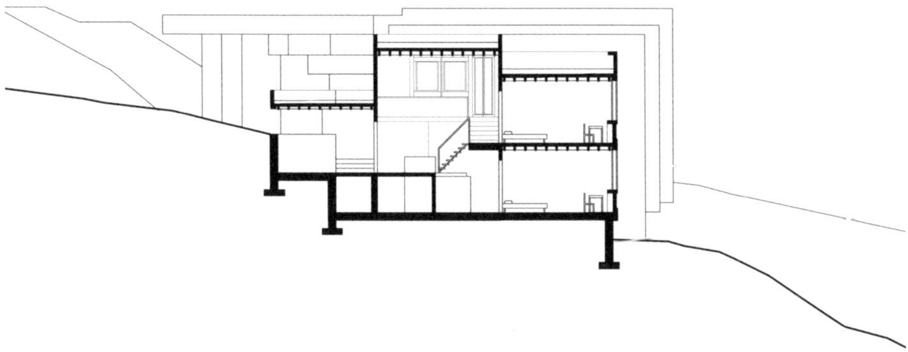

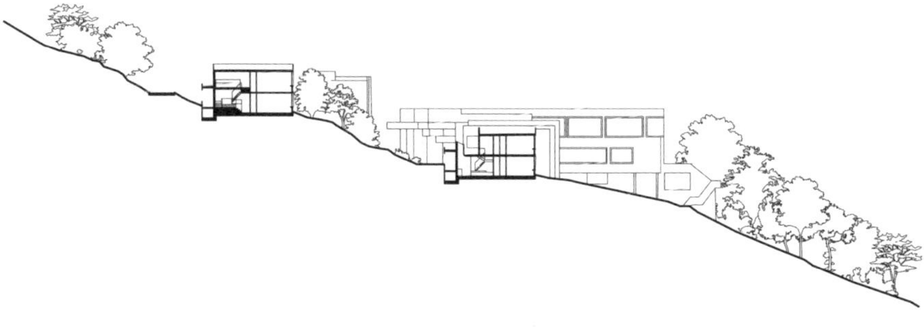

**with different levels of privacy. Built in parallel, and as an extension to Tridente, Serpentine has 152 single rooms divided into three blocks. These blocks appear to reproduce the jagged parallel rows of the Collegio del Colle nearby, and they comprise six (or seven) units, each with eight single rooms over two levels. The Serpentine dorms do not have a service building, so the rooms have slightly larger common areas. A double-height dining room is connected to a kitchenette and shared bathroom, and each unit has a private terrace on the roof. Across the street is the Aquilone residence, a linear**

---

**7 Aquilone**

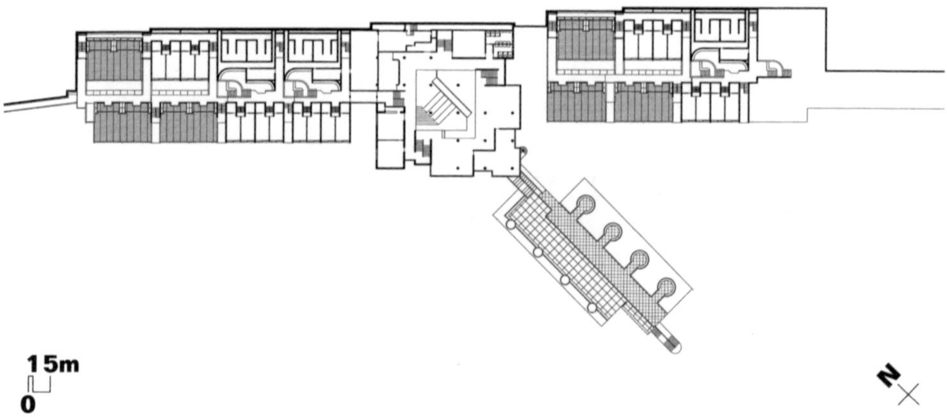


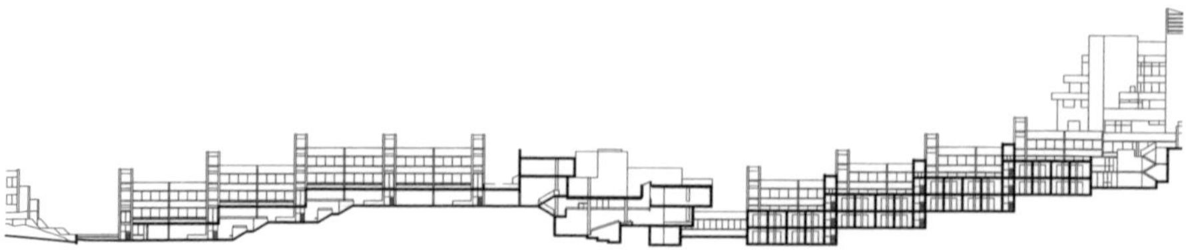

**building with two stepping rows of residences and a central service building. The central five-storey building with a square plan is an intricate maze of open floors that combine different common spaces. The main access is from the pedestrian bridge leading to the roof terrace. Whereas the lower floors were always reserved for the students, the upper floors were supposed to provide public functions open to the townspeople as well: ultimately, however, the restaurants, bars, cinema and shops were not realised and most of the redundant spaces are today used as storage. A four-storey library attached to the**

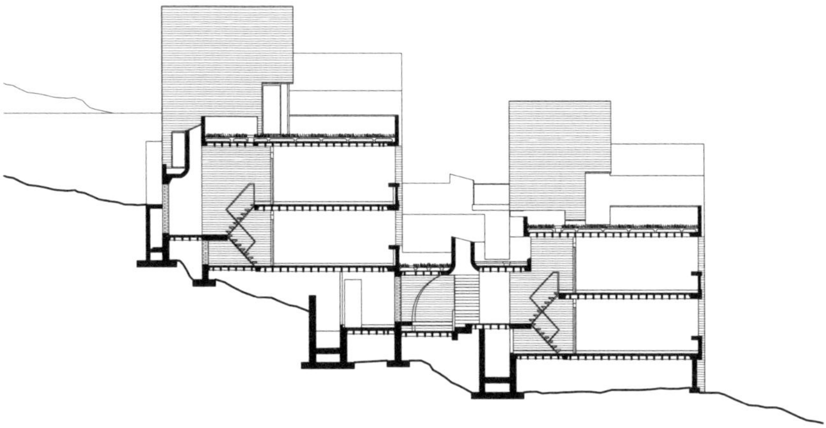

**corner of the central building can be accessed separately. The central service building is flanked by two residential wings divided into 16 blocks, each with 8 double rooms, accommodating a total of 256 students. All the rooms have access to a central linear roof garden with integrated skylights that illuminate the corridors below. The long narrow corridors are occasionally interrupted by pockets of common areas with integrated furniture. This interior scheme was multiplied in Vela, the remnant of the original, more ambitious scheme for Block A, which was intended to be twice its current size.**

---

**8 Vela**

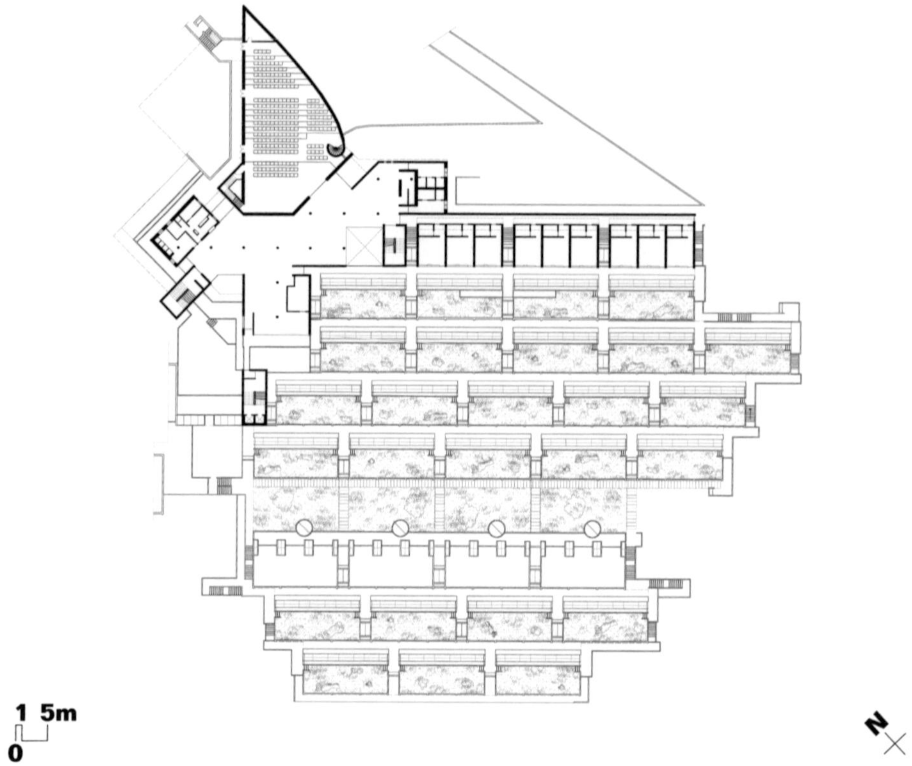

**The densest of all the residences, Vela has 156 single rooms and 33 double rooms, arranged in blocks of either six (single rooms) or three (double rooms) to make terraced rows with accessible roof gardens. The narrow corridors in between are almost 100m long and, as in the Aquilone, they are illuminated by zenithal light and feature occasional niches with fixed furniture—concrete benches and tables—intended for socialising. An elevator tower rises above the residential block and connects it to the service building at the rear, with a theatre, performance stage and public areas which were supposed to be open to all.**

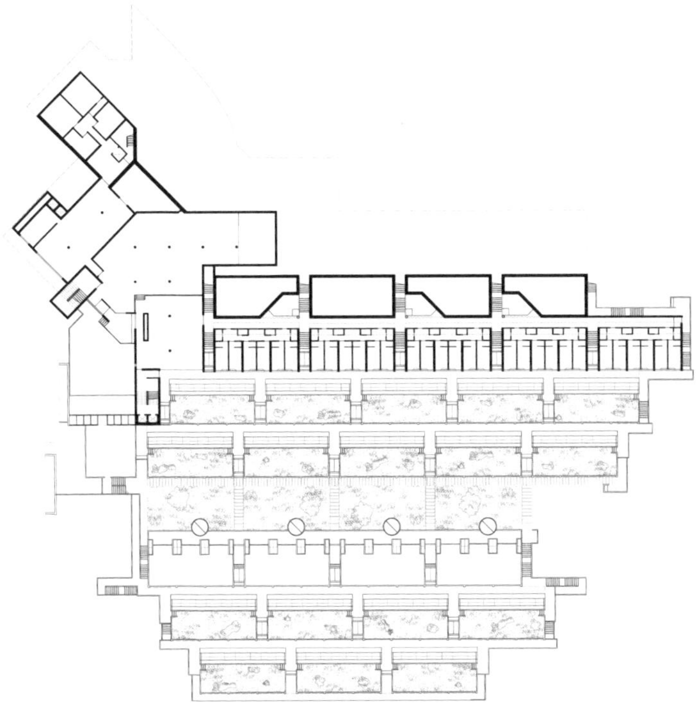

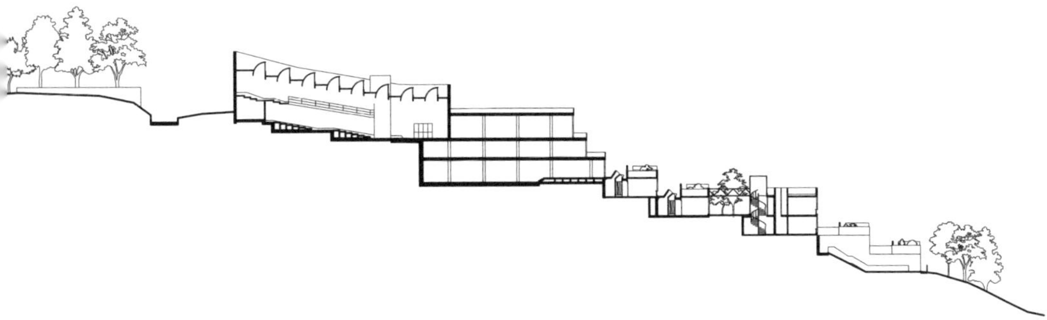

# Architecture of Good Intentions

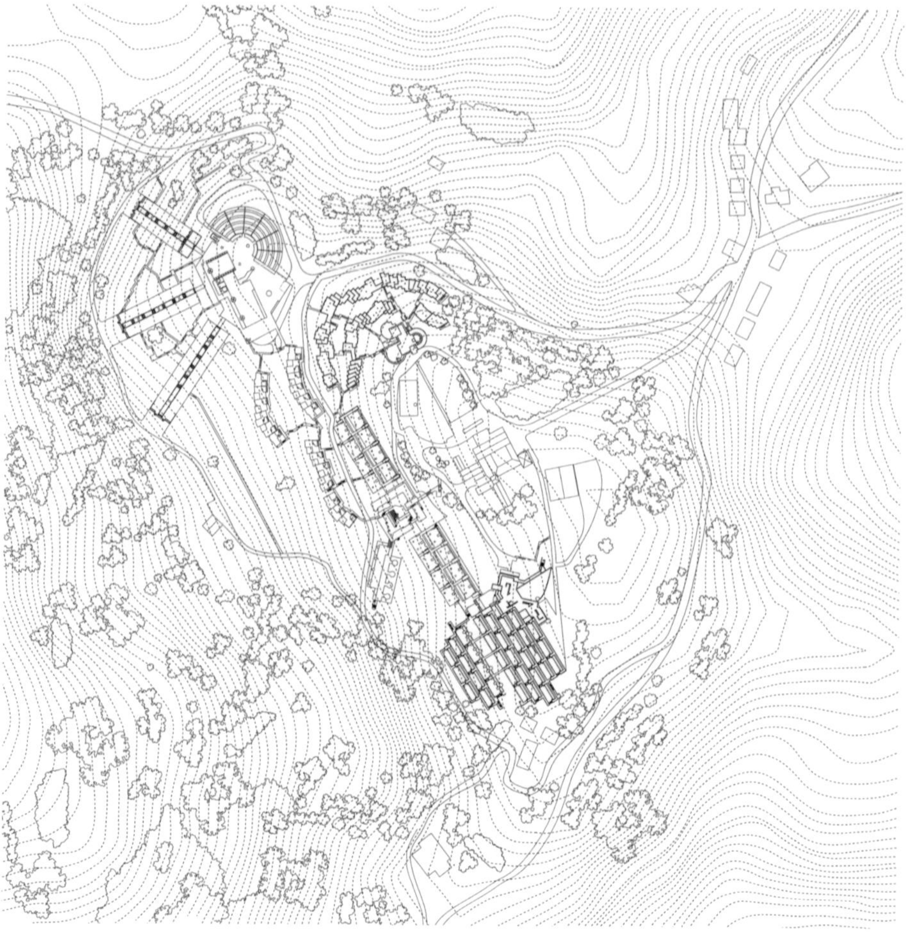

Urbino University campus

The era of mass demolition of the utopian social architecture from the 1960s and 1970s is long past. *Peak elimination time* was probably the late 1990s, when after two decades of discourse and debate a strange consensus was reached about the social ills allegedly unleashed by these structures. All of Giancarlo de Carlo's buildings in Urbino from the same era—which often share similar principles—curiously survived that day of reckoning. Why? There is no simple answer. Functioning essentially as an infrastructure for an endlessly transient population, none of the buildings suffered that fatal decline from a world fuelled by social promise to a parallel universe haunted by despair. Their combination of progressive ideology and successive generations of temporary, fundamentally powerless inhabitants ensured they could survive. Over time, the colleges came to represent a benevolent state apparatus that provided affordable housing for those willing to study, as some kind of idealisation of the *good society*. Inside the complexes, people are good, even if that means that they have to take a bus to town, with its auditoria, restaurants and bars, and be back home before eleven. Despite all of this, or perhaps because of it, the buildings endure.

Visiting these housing complexes today, one cannot shake the feeling of being in a place in its afterlife. The colleges look like some kind of archaeological site, discovered and laid bare, evidence of a former, more intelligent civilisation. A remarkable collection of architectural tropes, the city in the hills is mostly devoid of life, many of its figures and spaces somehow abandoned. But curiously, it is anything but deserted. The rooms are full, there is even a waiting list. What's happened? Phones and tablets have replaced the figments of public life, as the overload of echoing empty common spaces attests. Contemporary life does not happen in the endless underground adventure of corridors and niches, but in the various iterations of social media. The students—the inhabitants—are almost invisible, preferring the 'comfort' of their own rooms. This was obviously not what De Carlo intended. The DNA of the complexes—the increasingly erratic and, towards the end, monumental mazes of shared spaces paired with the reduced, and borderline uncomfortable, single rooms—seems to be constituted for and *towards* another era, another society, another humanity?

In a slightly perverse way, De Carlo's Urbino project shows the exact point at which architecture culture becomes visible; namely, the moment when its original function (its program) is put into question. When architecture is no longer needed but still stubbornly persists, it becomes tangible. Francesco di Giorgio's San Bernardino chapel, likewise outside the city walls of Urbino, shares a similar fate. It is visited almost solely for its curiously inverted interior architecture, an inner space defined by an internalised outer facade complete with windows and a frieze. We go there to see how its brick volumes protect some sort of frozen—and thus rescued—architecture inside. We visit the chapel without services, and the endless spaces of Di Carlo's delirium without social activities, and somehow we are astonished—perhaps excited even—that these spaces exist as some sort of token of good intentions, salvaged from the consequences of ideological posturing.

## Colophon

Giancarlo de Carlo
Experiments in Thickness

Everything Without
Content 233

Edited by
Kersten Geers,
Jelena Pančevac
Photographs
Stefano Graziani
Texts
Kersten Geers,
Jelena Pančevac
Copy editing
Pamela Johnston
Graphic Design
Joris Kritis
Drawings and
perspectives
Students of the
Academy of
Architecture USI,
Mendrisio (Spring
Semester 2023)
Cover
'Protest of the Youth'
installation by Giancarlo
de Carlo at the XIV
Triennale, photo by
Geert Bekaert, © Ghent
University, Faculty
Library, Engineering
and Architecture

Thanks to
Fondazione Ca'Romanino
Michael Meredith
Manuel Orazi
Véronique Patteeuw
Alessandra Spranzi
Christophe Van Gerrewey
David Van Severen
Andrea Zanderigo

Walter Angonese
Marco Della Torre
Academy of
Architecture USI,
Mendrisio

Academy of
Architecture USI,
Mendrisio

EVERYTHING
Kersten Geers

Guido Tesio
Fabrizio Ballabio

Spring Semester 2023
Tommaso Aliverti
Daria Baldovino
Vittoria Betti
Veronica Bissanti
Mauro Cecchetti
Vittorio Chiesa
Adele Cortese
Eliot Ferguen
Giambattista Ferro
Cara Naja Hähl-Pfeifer
Reneé Hendrix
Simão Jorge
Shuji Kambayashi
Nicolas Keldany
Simone Mirabella
Andrea Occelli
Alessandro Ostuni
Sofia Paganelli
Enrico Ricci
Nora Soldati
Joby Thoppil
Maria Turco
Andrea Vailati
Carolina Vanni

Printing
die Keure

Edition
1800 copies

Publisher
Verlag der
Buchhandlung Walther
und Franz König
Ehrenstr. 4
D–50672 Köln

Distribution

Germany, Austria and
Switzerland
Buchhandlung Walther
König
Ehrenstr. 4,
D–50672 Köln
T +49 (0)221/2059653
verlag@buchhandlung-walther-koenig.de

Unites States and
Canada
D.A.P. / Distributed
Art Publishers, Inc.
75 Broad Street,
Suite 630
USA – New York,
NY 10004
T +1 (0)2126271999
orders@dapinc.com

Outside the United
States and Canada,
Germany, Austria and
Switzerland by
Thames & Hudson Ltd.,
London
thamesandhudson.com

ISBN 978-3-7533-0578-3

Bibliographic information published by the Deutsche Nationalbibliothek. The Deutsche Nationalbibliothek lists this publication in the Deutsche Nationalbibliografie; detailed bibliographic data are available on the Internet at http://dnb.d-nb.de.

Printed in Belgium

Office Without Office
Kersten Geers
David Van Severen